D0425832

WOMEN AND THE SCIENTIFIC PROFESSIONS

The M.I.T. Symposium on American Women in Science and Engineering

WOMEN
AND THE SCIENTIFIC PROFESSIONS

The M.I.T. Symposium on American Women in Science and Engineering

EDITED BY

Jacquelyn A. Mattfeld and Carol G. Van Aken

THE M.I.T. PRESS

Massachusetts Institute of Technology
Cambridge, Massachusetts, and London, England

First M.I.T. Press Paperback Edition, June 1967

Library of Congress Catalog Card Number 65-26968
Printed in the United States of America

Foreword

On October 23 and 24, 1964, the Association of Women Students of the Massachusetts Institute of Technology sponsored a symposium which brought together a group of men and women, eminently qualified by training and interest, to discuss some of the problems faced by American women in scientific and engineering professions. A student committee, with the advice of members of the faculty, planned and organized the program for the delegates, who were women students from other colleges and universities, with an interest in a professional career in the sciences.

What began as a local meeting to consider only career possibilities and problems for M.I.T.'s women students quickly expanded into a national conference which was attended by 260 student delegates from 140 colleges, as well as about 600 guests—college deans, high school guidance counselors, women professionally employed in science, personnel managers, high school seniors, and the M.I.T. community. What began as a modest informational effort resulted in a fascinating exchange of ideas by distinguished and enthusiastic participants.

In planning the program and selecting the conference speakers, the committee considered the woman in the scientific profession from several points of view: from her own, from that of her immediate environment as represented by her family and her employer, and from that of the cultural environment as represented by society in general. The committee strove for a balanced presentation through the selection of participants with diverse outlooks—psychologists, sociologists, educators, employers, and women who are engaged in a scientific career.

Basically, the committee had three general purposes in mind in the organization of the symposium:

1. To acquaint girls seriously interested in a career in science and technological fields with the mythical and actual difficulties that they may expect to encounter, and to convey to them that these are not insurmountable, and that the satisfactions and rewards of such careers are high;

2. To bring together outstanding men and women, some already active in these fields, some in education and in industry, to focus their attention on the concerns of women preparing for careers in science and technology, in the hope that they may be stimulated to suggest new approaches and discover new solutions to the existing problems through discussion with the students and each other; and

3. To attract the favorable attention of industry, other educational institutions, and the public at large to the present successful contributions of women in these fields and to the desirability of decreasing the present barriers that now prevent maximum utilization of the abilities of qualified women in these areas.

It was the hope of the student committee that the Symposium would make it possible for a group of highly qualified and interested men and women to explore the personal, social, and economic factors involved in a woman's commitment to a scientific professional career, to report on the current status of women in industry and the academic world, to probe the problems associated with the employment of women, and to analyze a woman's prospects in these fields on the basis of the information presented. The papers presented in this volume are the result of this endeavor.

I should like to take this opportunity to acknowledge the generous contributions of time and effort made by innumerable members of the M.I.T. community, with particular thanks to my fellow workers on the student symposium committee, the faculty advisory committee, the Association of Women Students, the Association of M.I.T. Alumnae, and especially Dean Jacquelyn Mattfeld.

CAROL G. VAN AKEN

Cambridge, Massachusetts
June 11, 1965

Participants

Jessie Bernard

Professor of Sociology, The Pennsylvania State University

Bruno Bettelheim

Stella M. Rowley Professor of Education, University of Chicago

Richard H. Bolt

Chairman of the Board, Bolt Beranek and Newman Inc.; Lecturer in Political Science, Massachusetts Institute of Technology; Associate Director, National Science Foundation, 1960–63

Mary I. Bunting

President, Radcliffe College; Member, Atomic Energy Commission, 1964–65

Erik H. Erikson

Professor of Human Development and Lecturer on Psychiatry, Harvard University

Lillian M. Gilbreth

Management Consultant and Industrial Engineer; Webster-Mauzé Lecturer, Massachusetts Institute of Technology, 1964

Thomas W. Harrington, Jr.

Placement Officer, Massachusetts Institute of Technology

W. Scott Hill

Manager of Engineering Recruitment, General Electric Company

Marion G. Hogan

President, Weather Services, Inc.

Wilma A. Kerby-Miller

Radcliffe Dean for Graduate and Professional Women Students in Harvard University

James R. Killian, Jr.

Chairman of the Corporation, Massachusetts Institute of Technology

Rita McCabe

Director of Systems Personnel Programs, International Business Machines Corp.

Robert F. Mello

Director of College Relations and Recruitment, U.S. Civil Service Commission

Vivianne T. Nachmias

Research Associate in Anatomy, School of Medicine, University of Pennsylvania

Mina Rees

Dean of Graduate Studies, The City University of New York

Alice S. Rossi

Research Associate (Associate Professor), Committee on Human Development, University of Chicago

Dorothy M. Simon

Vice President and Director of Corporate Research, Avco Defense and Industrial Products Group

Julius A. Stratton

President, Massachusetts Institute of Technology

Carol G. Van Aken

Chairman, Symposium on American Women in Science and Engineering

Eleanor Webster

Chairman, Department of Chemistry, and Director, Institute in Chemistry, Wellesley College

Chien-Shiung Wu

Professor of Physics, Columbia University

WELCOMING REMARKS

JULIUS A. STRATTON

A conference at M.I.T. on science and engineering is hardly a novelty; but a symposium about women, on a campus that very likely you have thought to be a man's preserve, may well have appeared to you as something remarkable.

Yet we do not come wholly new to the field. For as your program notes will tell you, M.I.T. awarded its first degree to a woman student ninety-one years ago. Her name was Ellen Swallow. She was a graduate of Vassar College, and she came here to study chemistry. In the laboratories of the old brick buildings on Boylston Street, across the Charles, she began her distinguished career in science. To this day her happy and effective life symbolizes to us the achievements of the many women who have followed in her path.

Now the fact that Vassar and M.I.T. happen to have been founded in the same year—1861—is, of course, a pure coincidence. Neither could rightly claim to be the first institution of its kind. Nonetheless, though unlike one another in almost every respect, they did have more than Ellen Swallow in common: each had been created as an expression of a powerful new idea.

For Vassar, and for her sister colleges of the same era, many of which are represented here today, it was the belief that woman, "having received from her Creator the same intellectual constitution as man, has the same right as man to intellectual culture and development," a very bold proposition indeed in the middle of the nineteenth century.

And for M.I.T. it was the new idea that there is dignity and importance in the mastery of useful knowledge and that science and engineering can be the legitimate foundations of a higher education.

In the intervening years these institutions have grown and developed. But more importantly, the ideas for which they stood have also prospered.

On the one hand, women have sought and earned a place of their own in our society. They have ventured into every field, and they have been successful. And on the other, science and technology have penetrated into every domain of human affairs, opening a vast array of new opportunities for women as well as for men.

The overt purpose of this symposium on American women is to examine the present scene; to review the part played by women in the professions today; to identify the forces that are reshaping our society, the problems to be solved, the opportunities that are emerging, and the needs that must be fulfilled.

But underlying this conference there is for us at M.I.T. an even further and deeper significance. For this meeting here on our campus is testimony to our commitment to the education of women. We understand and support the expanding role of women in industry, in teaching, in research, and indeed in government—and their desire to participate on a larger scale. We believe, moreover, that an institution of this character, with its special resources for science and engineering—and for all the related fields of architecture, management, economics, political science—has a particular responsibility toward this end.

Our commitment is evident in many ways. There is tangible evidence in our new McCormick Hall. It should be clear from our rapidly increasing enrollment of women as undergraduates and as candidates for graduate degrees. And there is evidence, above all, in the way in which the women students are accepted into the life of this community on a completely equal footing with men.

And now, finally, to these women students I should like to pay a special tribute. For this symposium is the product of their ideas and their initiative, and it was their hard work that has made it a reality. It is with pride and satisfaction in their accomplishment—as well as with gratitude to the speakers who have so willingly joined in our efforts—that I welcome you most warmly today.

Contents

PART I

The Commitment Required of a Woman Entering a Scientific Profession

THE COMMITMENT REQUIRED OF A WOMAN ENTERING A SCIENTIFIC PROFESSION IN PRESENT-DAY AMERICAN SOCIETY

BRUNO BETTELHEIM

Panel Discussion

MARY I. BUNTING, *Moderator*

Panelists

RITA MCCABE

VIVIANNE T. NACHMIAS

MINA REES

DOROTHY M. SIMON

CHIEN-SHIUNG WU

THE COMMITMENT REQUIRED OF A WOMAN ENTERING A SCIENTIFIC PROFESSION IN PRESENT-DAY AMERICAN SOCIETY

Bruno Bettelheim

I am grateful to you for the honor you have bestowed on me by inviting me to participate in this conference. That you have asked me, a man, and one whose experience is far removed from the physical sciences and engineering, to give the opening address overawes me. This symposium deals with a problem of such magnitude, and with such far-reaching implications, that my contribution cannot possibly do justice to it. I imagine that you have asked me to speak on this topic because you wish to stress the psychological issues involved in a woman's entering the scientific professions, that is, those issues pertaining to her being a woman who does so. To these specific aspects of the problem I shall hence address myself.

Therefore I am happy that this symposium is not simply a symposium on the commitment required of any person entering the scientific profession, but rather that required of a woman who enters it. It focuses our attention on a fact so basic that, because of its obviousness, it tends to be disregarded in the everyday business of preparing for a profession. What could be more self-evident than the proposition that men are men, and women women, and since they are all human beings they have similar aspirations and hopes for self-fulfillment? Yet how difficult it is to draw from these facts conclusions for all our daily activities. Again, what could be more obvious than that women are not men? But all too often we pay scant attention to our realization of this difference — especially when it comes to woman's role in the professions.

Of course, there is no female or male way to solve the engineering problems involved in building a dam, or in planning electric generators. But different persons feel differently about working on the designing or building of a dam, though the end results of their efforts may show no difference. Although men and women may be equally able to solve a problem in physics or engineering, I believe that, while they do so, they will experience characteristically male or female emotions about their work, ways of feeling that have nothing to do with its quality, or with its results. Now, given the tremendously wide variations that are found among people, there will always be some women who feel about their work in very much the way that seems typical of men, and there are men whose emotional approach to their work and its execution is very much like that typical of women. But these are and should be the exceptions rather than the rule.

There were two reasons why I accepted your kind invitation to talk to you today, though I knew it might put me out on a limb. The first was my desire to stress this difference in feeling, though the result may not show it. The second and more important reason is that I was not asked to speak about women as scientists, but of their commitment to becoming scientists. Commitment is a feeling, not a hard fact, and with feelings I feel at home. Science and engineering having been for many generations a masculine domain, so it seems understandable that women, having only recently entered these professions, must have feelings about doing so. Because scientific problems and tasks are identical for men and women, since they depend, not on the sex of the worker, but on the nature of the problem, there is the pitfall that women may try to deny that they have feelings, womanly feelings, about these problems and may repress them and try to approach these tasks with the same emotional attitudes that men have who for generations have been active in these fields of study and achievement. But this should and need not be so. And to disregard their specific female feelings about these tasks can be to the detriment not only of the job at hand, but also of the possibility of recruiting a large number of women for these important tasks.

Science and engineering have been the endeavors of men for so long that it is understandable that the first women who entered these fields were often women who in many ways felt more like men than the rest of their sex. Wishing to do well in their chosen field, to show their mettle in competition with men, they tended also to embrace masculine attitudes toward their work, though neither masculine nor feminine attitudes are required for research or engineering, but only those in line with the essential nature of the problem. While understandable for historic reasons, I believe that to continue to think along these lines is a disservice to men and women, to science, and to engineering.

Since men and women are different from each other in their emotional make-up, womanly emotional attitudes to these professions are as legitimate as are male emotional attitudes. As I hope to suggest later, it is to the advantage of the results if all human tasks are approached not only in the rational ways in which they must be approached, and which will be identical for males and females, but also with emotional attitudes that may be different for males than for females. Only if this becomes common practice will many more females enter these fields and work happily in them.

Here I must confess that I will have to enlarge on my topic. I know little about the specifics of the sciences (aside from the social sciences) or about requirements for employment in such fields as physics, mathematics, and engineering. But I am convinced that the problems of women scientists are not essentially different from those of all professional women. So with your permission I shall speak of the professional woman in general, of the difficulties she faces, of what she may reasonably expect of society and society of her, and of those changes we need to effect in our present world to do justice to both woman's aspirations as a human being and her aspirations as a woman.

I believe that any woman's most important commitment is to being a woman. Such a commitment should embrace all the activities of her life: her life as a wife and mother, her work in the laboratory or research institute, her role in society. Let me illustrate with an example from Laurens van der Post's new book, A *View of all the Russias.*[1] Like others before him, Van der Post describes how in Russia women work alongside men in all fields of work. As an example he tells about a young Russian girl who volunteered to work for three years in Siberia on the building of the

[1] New York: Morrow, 1964.

huge dam and hydroelectric works at Bratsk. This young lady fell in love with her work, with its excitement and what it meant as a contribution to the betterment of all men. She decided to stay on and to become an engineer by combining her studies with her work and — this is my point — with her private life as a woman. She loved her work, or, if you prefer, in the sense of my title, she felt a commitment to it. But she loved it as a young woman would, not in the manner of a young man. Though she may have been as competent a worker as her male co-workers, this does not mean that she was "one of the boys." Her commitment was a female one because the essence of her emotions was female; her personal way of loving her work was a womanly embracing of her tasks rather than a masculine conquering of them.

Russian society is, of course, different from American. But only after we have accepted, as have the Russians, the position that engineering is not a male profession will we be ready to arrange things so that the female commitment to a scientific task will be as valuable as that of a man. I suggest, in fact, that there are no essentially male or essentially female professions, that all are human professions and that they can become more human as we allow men and women to make their essentially human, but specifically male or female, contribution.

In Russia today the main commitment seems to be to a task to be mastered. Little conscious effort is made to master it the better by having men contribute to it in specifically masculine ways and women in specifically feminine ways. Yet this is what we need. We need to concentrate on the particular task's human challenge, by giving conscious recognition to the fact that any task requires the synthesis of the male and the female spirit in its achievement.

Let me give you another example, this time from my own field. In our work with severely disturbed children, we do not find it too difficult to find women committed to working for and with these psychotic youngsters. They bring a female kind of love and dedication to their task. This is as one would expect. Our problem lies with recruiting male workers. It is much harder to find equally dedicated males, though one does find some. But the trouble with most of them is that they are committed to their work in too feminine a way. This just will not do. The reason for the difficulty, however, has to do with the way in which we stereotype professional activities. To most of the young men in my line of work it is not clear that there is and must be a typically masculine type of commitment to the care of disturbed children. They try instead to commit themselves to the work in a female spirit. But the rehabilitation of the children — both boys and girls — requires the help of dedicated therapists, both male and female. We never find enough male workers, though, and certainly not enough male workers who go about their jobs in a genuinely masculine way. By this I do not mean rough and ready sporting types, but men who can care and nurture in as gentle and emphatic a masculine way as women can in a feminine spirit.

I hope it is obvious by now that my idea of commitment to a profession has nothing to do with considerations such as society's need for trained manpower. Such a necessity may or may not exist for a country at a particular moment in history. For example, the idea seems to be a main motivation in current Russian policies. On the contrary, I believe that all human beings, if they are to be committed to their work, need the conviction that what they do is intrinsically important, that to do it is important to them, regardless of the needs of others or of society, though this also enters because what we do is enhanced in our eyes if we also feel that through our job we make a significant contribution. But to work at what is important to us — rather than to others — forms part of our finding personal fulfillment, as women if we are women, as men if we are men. My concern is with the human aspects of the problem of commitment to one's life work, and not at all with particular skills or what it is asserted are the needs of society.

This is not to say that our society does not need professional skills. Of course it does. But unless one feels a deep personal urge to meet those needs, one is degraded to the level of a tool serving exterior purposes. To realize one's human potential, one cannot be a mere tool but should always be a person, engaging only in those activities that further one's development as a human being. Now, few people are so insensitive to the real needs of society that they do not feel the personal challenge to work for the well-being of society and with it to lift their activities out of the solipsistic to the social level. This is fortunate, because only in this way can the needs of society be met in personally satisfying ways.

But there still remain barriers to the mutually beneficial interacting of the human being and his society. One of them is our tendency to view man and society in terms of competition, of economic production and rewards. I do not believe, for instance, that we are trying to reach the moon because our competition with the communist world requires it. If that were our only incentive, we should not succeed. We shall do so only if people are fired by their personal imagination, by their personal wish to transcend the limitations of their terrestrial existence. Personally I feel no challenge in such an enterprise — this is why I am not in the field of engineering. But I believe that I have empathy with those who respond to that particular challenge and are impelled by it. I think I can understand what such a commitment means to them and to their growth as persons, and that such a commitment exists irrespective of what success may mean to the power and glory of America. I have a similar investment in the exploration of the so-far uncharted inner world of man. I feel the challenge of that unknown — if you like, of that nether world — and I find personal satisfaction and enrichment from my feeling that perhaps I have managed a further step beyond what I have already known or experienced. And this is not because society needs it — though I hope that in some infinitely small way society also may benefit from it — but because it satisfies me.

All this suggests that, if we wish to have a meaningful life, we must make our work part of it, and of our life's meaning. I am afraid, though, that that is a truism all too easily accepted rather than lived by. We go off the track when we commit ourselves, let us say, to engineering as such, rather than to the most deeply human essence of the particular engineering task. Take the example of teaching. Russian psychological thinking is, as you know, based on conditioning theories. To view man as motivated mainly by automatic responses also has its adherents among us, as a matter of fact even as close as a neighboring campus. Professor Skinner, for example, has offered an explanation of the teaching process. He asks why, indeed, students study at all, and supplies us with the answer that they do it to avoid the consequences of not studying. I do not find that a very satisfactory answer. Certainly it runs counter to what every true teacher since Socrates — and probably long before him — has known from his own experience. To let

Goethe speak for all of them, "One never learns to understand truly anything but what one loves" ("*Man lernt nichts kennen als was man liebt*"). A teacher committed to teaching children, rather than pigeons, knows that the only effective and enduring motivation for study lies in its pleasures and the excitement of learning what, because of this personal involvement, becomes deeply meaningful to oneself. Only if one loves teaching can one teach well; only if one loves learning can one learn well. And only if one loves scientific work can one achieve meaning through it, as opposed to earning money from it. If you want to be able to love scientific or engineering work, you must be able to view it apart from economic production and reward, because only then can you and will you be committed to it.

That we in the western world can afford to put economic considerations out of our mind, we owe to the technicians, scientists, engineers. For that we owe them deep gratitude. Only because they have created for the rest of us a society of abundance can we all afford to work for greater purposes than securing mere survival. We can, for example, stop thinking of education in terms of greater earning power, because nothing is more destructive to education for human purposes than is education for economic gain. If we think of college education as a means of fitting us for a job, or ensuring a higher income, that is all it will yield. And for too many people this is all they get out of college. Nothing is more alien to the good life than to make man fit for a job when the real problem is to make the job fit for man — or, in the present context, fit for a wife and mother.

Often the problems of professional women are put in economic terms: should they or should they not work to increase the economic well-being of society; or should they or should they not devote themselves to the task of *pro-*

ducing high-quality children (in Professor Parson's terms), as opposed to simply having them. Yet what is radically new in our human opportunities is exactly the fact that neither the family nor society need be geared toward production any more, neither of material goods nor of children.

The problem of woman's role in our age of technology is hardly new. Its essential solution was stated firmly a century and a half ago when Balzac recognized that "A woman who has had a man's education is the possessor of both the most brilliant faculties and the faculties most fruitful in happiness both for herself and for her husband." Thus Balzac knew that the educated woman through her education becomes more of a woman, and not more like a man. Times have changed since then, because today the education of most women matches that of their husbands. But beyond that we have not progressed very much. Because as far as her "brilliant faculties" are concerned, although we develop them through education, more often than not they are then permitted to lie fallow. At least most men seem uncomfortable about living with a woman who makes use of her brilliant faculties outside the home, and quite a few women seem reluctant to use them. Among the reasons for this is a widespread feeling that, if a mother uses her abilities and creates a full life for herself outside the home, she is cheating her children, if not also her husband, despite what Balzac believed.

In a strange dialectic process, the same insights of psychoanalysis that helped to unfetter the Victorian woman have imposed new restraints. Having broken the shackles that kept her from freely using her faculties, and having helped us to understand the psychological reasons for the shackles in the first place, they have created brand-new worries for the woman who wants to think well of herself as a mother.

Because psychoanalysis has made us so aware of the emotional needs of children, it is now the conscientious woman who frets excessively about her infant, ready to meet his every need; later she feels she must always be available to her child, to protect him from overstimulation, understimulation, and to take care of him lovingly at all moments. In short, her faculties are highly developed, and she wants to use them to the full, but she worries that to do so beyond the confines of the home means deserting her children, if not also her husband. This is her dilemma.

It is also why the conjugal happiness that Balzac foresaw would result from equal education of the sexes seems somehow to elude many of the couples so endowed. But all this need not be. So let us speculate a bit about what has gone wrong, what kind of changes are needed, and what may be done to effect them.

First let us discuss the erroneous idea that the working wife and mother is a modern invention. On the contrary, the full-time wife and mother is a phenomenon that only modern technology has made possible. Before the industrial revolution and except for ruling groups of insignificant number, both men and women of all societies not based on slavery had to be active in the economic process if the family was to prosper. The pioneer woman, and later the wife of the farmer, the small artisan, and the shopkeeper was usually as fully involved in the economic and social activities of the family as her husband. The lives of both husband and wife moved within the small circle of village life in which both were an integral part. Their worlds were not separated, either socially or economically, or spiritually; nor was the world of adults set apart from children. Such a life was far from idyllic. Labor was cruel, life was full of anxieties, and amenities were few. But people shared it and were rarely alone in their struggle. Their very existence depended on working together.

If working for sheer survival formed the essence of life, then they had a full life. And this is what counts in terms of human satisfaction, whether the things we are doing seem to be the most meaningful things we can possibly do. If they are, we attain self-realization whether we call this human integration, or autonomy, or self-actualization, or an access to peak experience.

Obviously no self-realization is possible unless man has mastered his two greatest tasks: first, self-preservation, which in our present world includes not only preservation of the existing population but also extending the scope of our mass technological society; and, second, the procreation of the species. Of these two tasks the first has been more the domain of the male, the second of the female. At the same time, no full self-realization was possible for either sex without active participation in both tasks. Thus while man's principal means of self-realization was through work, he could not achieve it without his role as husband and father becoming central to the meaning of his life. Woman's parallel path to autonomy lay in being wife and mother. But unless she, too, had a meaningful share in the work of preserving the present generation and of extending the horizons of future generations, procreation alone was not enough to fill out the meaning of her life. Before birth control the more numerous pregnancies certainly made her fully aware of her procreative role. That she was also worn out by these pregnancies as much as by physical and economic hardships is here beside the point. What is significant is that only technological advances (less physical hardship in production) and scientific progress (control of pregnancies) permit both sexes today to find self-realization in ways they have chosen and not ways that are forced on them by necessity.

To a large degree the problems facing professional women stem from the fact that these women are expected today to enter a masculinely oriented working world as men, so to speak. They have all too little chance to enter a world that is at least as organized for the requirements of working women as it is for the requirements of the machine, or technology, or a science whose requirements are viewed as independent of the inner needs of the men and women who pursue them.

To remedy this we must start with the realization that, as much as women want to be good scientists or engineers, they want first and foremost to be womanly companions of men and to be mothers. In our thinking on working mothers the attitude seems to be that it is their motherhood that must somehow be fitted into their working life. Knowing that this runs counter to their natural desires, many women give up trying to fit work into their prime concern with motherhood. Well-intentioned efforts to encourage women to continue in their profession after their children are fairly grown only sidestep the issue, because they start with the assumption that the two — work and motherhood — are not really compatible. And they are not, unless work and child care are so arranged that neither childhood nor motherhood suffers.

A felicitous arrangement would require as a minimum: shorter working hours for the mothers of young children, work close to their home, excellent professional care for their children during the at-first four and later six hours these women would spend at work away from home, and ready availability of the mother to her children in the event of emergency.

Such arrangements presuppose an entirely different attitude toward work. They require that we free ourselves of the idea that this is still a life where we are just a hairsbreadth away from starvation. I have written a whole book[2] to show how modern man has actually perished because he is still fettered to economic thinking that belongs to the preindustrial era. I was referring to those who were so tied to their earthly possessions that they were too bogged down to escape Hitler's holocaust. Since the beginning of time man has lived in scarcity. Now for the first time, modern technology has done away with scarcity, or has the potential to do so. But scarcity thinking dies slow. Even while we busily plan for change, we persist in our psychological blindness to changes that are already fact.

Let me illustrate with the fetish of efficiency. It was the efficiency of modern technology that made us rich. But now that we are rich, we need not sacrifice to this god any more. We can afford to take our work at a more leisurely pace. If we do, we will not need to escape from work or fight for shorter hours or for more leisure time that we do not know how to fill. When labor is backbreaking, there is no point in stretching it out; the sooner it is completed the better. But labor need not be backbreaking any more. With monotonous work, too, there is no point in taking it more slowly; it only stretches out the hours of monotony. But labor need not be monotonous, if we do not sacrifice to efficiency at all cost. By using our full potential of workers, male and female, young and old, we could produce all the goods and services they could reasonably require. We could do it by making allowances for the need to humanize work: by making it companionable, unexhausting, diversified, and

[2] *The Informed Heart: Autonomy in a Mass Age*. New York: The Free Press of Glencoe, 1960.

satisfying in itself, beyond the wages it brings. If we do this, I believe we shall also have gone a long way toward controlling the population explosion. Women who also find satisfaction in work will not have to produce large numbers of children as their only means of satisfaction. It is not the professional woman who sets six or more children into the world.

Radical as are the changes in attitude I am suggesting, they are only the first steps in the humanization of work that modern technology permits. They are only preconditions for the most important change of all: to arrange work in line with the psychological nature of man which, at different times of his life, is very different. Thanks to mass production and automation, we have new freedoms now, in arranging our work within the human dimension. These would permit us to change the nature of what a man or woman is working on, in line with the life style of his age group and sex. Most people find that the same work, after a number of years, becomes monotonous, however intrinsically interesting at first. They find new excitement in changing the nature of their work after the old work activity has gone stale. Also, there is work of a character and rhythm that comes naturally to a young person, and entirely different work that comes naturally to an old one. There is work that comes naturally to a young woman before she has borne her own children, other work that suits her best when her children are young, and still other work when her children are grown.

But there is another human dimension to work that we have only begun to recognize. Professor Erikson has recently brought to our attention psychological corroboration of the age-old feeling that men and women are drawn to master different areas of living. Women feel more comfortable in dealing with problems of life that unfold within well-defined space; they are masters in exploring and fulfilling the requirements of living within an "inner space" of experience. Men are equally drawn to mastery of external space (which only incidentally includes stellar space but pertains chiefly to mastery over nature at large).[3]

I do not believe that our present work arrangements do justice to man's specific genius for conquering, changing, adapting nature to his needs, or for organizing society and pushing open new frontiers. Certainly they do not do justice to woman's specific genius for nurturing, humanizing, preserving. Society certainly needs a new ordering of life where, in all spheres, the domestic as well as the social world at large, these specific endowments of the sexes are encouraged to influence the flavor of all human settings and activities.

I wish I knew more about physics and engineering, so that perhaps I could spell out for you how the specific female genius can find its realization in these particular fields of human endeavor. But I do know, for example, that the building of houses, of our homes, has been entrusted far too much to a masculine thinking about structure and material. Our planning and building of houses has, in my opinion, lagged far behind our building of bridges, for example, for this very reason. Homes that are planned with the children's playroom relegated to the basement and with kitchens designed along the line of chemical laboratories show none of the impact of the female genius for mothering, for caring, for cooking for her family. Picture windows looking out on nothing in particular reflect the masculine genius for looking and reaching into the distance, and none of the female genius for creating an intimate atmosphere, which alone en-

[3] Erik Erikson, "Reflections on Womanhood," *Daedalus*, Spring 1964.

courages the growth and fulfillment of close human relations. The efficient high-rise public housing is a monument to a male concern with problems of engineering, but because the female genius is lacking these structures make it impossible to create homes in which children can grow up to become successful adults.

I hope these examples may serve to illustrate why I believe we deeply need women scientists and engineers who are committed, as human beings and as good workers, to their profession, and who are committed to it in line with their female genius.

❡ *Panel Discussion*

THE COMMITMENT REQUIRED OF A WOMAN ENTERING A SCIENTIFIC PROFESSION

MARY I. BUNTING, *Moderator*

Our assignment this morning is to discuss women's commitment to scientific professions, the investment they are able and willing to make, the factors, genetic and environmental, that influence their commitment, its significance to them, to science, and to society. This is a broad topic, subject to many approaches and interpretations.

Some of the panelists may wish to analyze the experiences of those women who have in fact undertaken scientific careers. If so, we should bear in mind how small the number entering science has been in this country. A small stream can be diverted readily; the river sweeps obstructions aside. The significant differences will not be found by comparing stream and river molecules, or by enumerating the diversions encountered by the stream.

Other panelists may be more concerned with what can be done to arouse the scientific interest of greater numbers of women — the untapped reservoir with its genetically sorted distribution of potentially productive gene combinations. Recent National Merit studies indicate that girls have in fact been more responsive than boys to the post-Sputnik push. What does this signify, if true?

Hopefully our discussions will enlarge our understanding of the commitment of men as well as women, and of commitment to other disciplines as well as to the sciences. But our chances of formulating fruitful hypotheses will be improved, I believe, by giving careful attention to the particularities of women and of science, rather than by ignoring them. I am fond of pointing out that the vitamins so essential to human nutrition were not discovered until physiologists attempted to maximize the growth of rats, chicks, and even bacteria. It is encouraging that educators are at last beginning to consider the educational requirements of special groups such as females in science or children of poverty.

To my mind, the distinctive elements in a woman's career are functions of her family responsibilities. She is particularly apt to encounter interruptions in midstream and to be limited in her choice of geographic location. These elements pose special difficulties in the more advanced and fast-moving scientific professions because science is additive and because scientific success often depends on access to special equipment and colleagues. However, achievement in the sciences is a complex phenomenon. We rationalize the stunning advances made by younger mathematicians in terms of what they do not know. Let us test rather than prejudge the woman in her forties; she may have some of the same assets.

Facts and theories in the social sciences, and I include education, must be handled with great caution. They have a way of entering the field of observation through the back door. Thus, a small statistical difference between the sexes in mathematical aptitudes is used all too often to counsel even extraordinarily able girls from planning careers in mathematics or the physical sciences. The implications of the fact that one is dealing with differences between huge populations that are largely overlapping are not sufficiently appreciated, not to mention the fact that people with quite different kinds of attitudes make worthwhile contributions in mathematics, or with it. The statistical fallacy is relatively easy to spot for those with scientific training; we may not be so alert to qualitative statements about sex differences that are used in similar cyclical arguments.

I decided many years ago that I was far more interested in being a fact than in living anyone else's theory.

Whether, given the information now at hand, women should be advised to enter some fields of science rather than others is a matter for judgment. Madame Curie chose to do her thesis on radium because it was of so little interest to her competitors — her fellow graduate students, you know — that she thought she could manage it at her own pace along with her family responsibilities. All investigators make choices about points of attack, depending on their capabilities, interests, and opportunities. This is quite a different thing from external limitation or regulation, which may be based on criteria that, at least in a proper environment, could become irrelevant, such as family income, sex, or full-time availability.

My plea, as you listen today and later as you ask, is for an experimental approach. What can be done to maximize the continuities in a woman's life? How serious need the interruptions be if, instead of considering them reasons for rejection, we accept them as interesting challenges. What would be the effects of introducing greater flexibility in women's education and employment? To date, this country has, in my opinion, proceeded on the theory that one does not really expect any significant contribution from women in science. Therefore, why struggle? This is a perfectly reasonable hypothesis but not, until it is more carefully tested, a trustworthy conclusion. We need to test it — to obtain an adequate sample, to provide an environment optimum for women, and to observe results — before using it to guide the planning of women's education and their employment in the sciences.

Let us, therefore, try to devise some good alternative hypothesis relating to this question that can be tested decisively, even though we may have to start on the outer edges. On the basis of a few, very small experiments that I have instigated, I have reason to think that such an approach might reveal some pertinent facts quite rapidly.

For example, when Douglass College admitted married women as part-time students and when the Radcliffe Institute offered assistance to women with families who wished to pursue advanced projects on a part-time basis, it soon became apparent that those who applied were very highly committed to their respective disciplines. But education and employment practices had ordinarily ruled such women out, perhaps because part-time men had often proved unsatisfactory. These women had thus been rejected, and conclusions about women's commitment had been drawn only after they had been discarded. If highly committed women were dropped permanently because of temporary irregularities due to family responsibilities, why would a girl choose such a career?

Our society is changing in many ways, not the least of which is in the diversity of opportunities opening in the sciences. Women's lives have been equally affected. Without doubt our theories influence the opportunities we offer and the commitments we encourage. These are not independent variables. The danger is that outmoded theories may condition present action and lead to quite false conclusions.

Once again, my plea is for an experimental approach, fully recognizing how difficult this is to achieve in dealing with human relations and human commitments. But it is essential to a better understanding. It is the contribution one would hope for over the years at many levels and along many fronts — educational, vocational, family, community. It is the contribution that this university and those in this audience would seem especially qualified to make.

RITA McCABE, *Panelist*

I feel very honored to be included in this panel since I am not an engineer, a scientist, or a mathematician; I am probably unique in this group, having majored in psychology. But I have been in the business world for a long time and have worked closely with scientists and engineers and particularly with women in business for many years.

The area that I represent is not an established profession of long standing, but a comparatively new field — the field of computers and data processing. It is also an area in which a considerable number of women have been accepted and have made significant contributions.

In recent years, as you know, the computer has moved far beyond its traditional areas of application. As these advances have taken place, a new profession has sprung up within the computer industry. It may be called systems design or systems analysis. In IBM we call it systems engineering.

Systems engineering, in relation to data processing, means solving problems with computers. It is the job of the systems engineer to find solutions to data-processing problems. This involves a variety of steps, first of which is determining what is the problem to be solved. Once you define the problem, you usually develop several different solutions, using mathematical techniques, logical techniques, procedural techniques, or maybe a combination of all of them. Then you must decide which is the best solution to this problem, and you must also specify the computer system to be used for a specific problem. There are many computers today, of all sizes and with many different input and output units. So it is quite a job to decide which system can best solve a particular problem. After the problem has been defined, the best solution has been worked out to solve the problem, and the computer has been specified, then you can develop plans for testing, installing, and operating the system.

This is the job of the systems engineer, and systems engineers are found in all computer manufacturing companies and in all companies and institutions that use computers, although the name "systems engineer" is not always used. There are quite a few women in systems engineering. Our company alone has over one thousand college women in this field throughout the country, and we have another 180 women in Europe who are nationals of their countries. These women are helping companies, organizations, and institutions solve their data-processing problems with computers.

Another large area associated with computers is programming. Most people have a little familiarity with programming these days. They know that the computers will do nothing until someone tells them what to do. Programming is the art of writing a series of instructions in such form that the machine is able to act on them.

Of course, there are many other jobs associated with the computer field. However, the two areas that I have described are significant because many women have been accepted in these areas and have made significant contributions.

How did women get into this new field? One of the primary reasons was the shortage of qualified people, and this shortage still exists. Even though many of the people currently in the computer industry have a diversity of educational backgrounds, the companies first sought, are still seeking, and will continue to seek mathematicians, engineers, and scientists for this work. The reason is that computers are being used more and more for complex problems involving simulation, management science, data transmission, information retrieval, and so forth. And these new application areas require a high level of technical skills.

As for the difficulties that women face in the computer world, I think they are similar to those they face in other areas. There are certainly prejudices about women in business, and very often their reception depends upon the men in charge. Some men accept women, others do not. It is no different from the time when Plato thought that women should enjoy equality in the arts and culture with the men, and Aristotle did not. This conflict still remains today. However, women are much more apt to be accepted in an area where there is a shortage of people, and this has been the case in the computer industry.

Promotional opportunities in the computer world do not come as fast for women as they do for men, but they are increasing gradually. There are many reasons why promotions for women have lagged. Very often promotion means relocation. Are women likely to be willing to give up their homes or apartments and move to another part of the country? Many of them are not. Often there is an excessive amount of travel involved with a certain position, or long hours. This matter of hours is a real problem. Even though there are laws that specify equal pay for women in some situations, there are many state laws that restrict the working hours for women.

The number of women holding managerial jobs in the computer world is very small. I do not believe that this number will grow very fast because I think it takes an unusual woman to manage men as well as women. There are some women who have done an excellent job.

As far as satisfactions and rewards for women are concerned, I think that the computer industry offers many — the satisfaction of teaching someone how to program a computer, the satisfaction of helping to develop a new programming language, the satisfaction of finding better ways to solve problems. In this area there are new problems all the time, new applications for computers, new computers to learn. There is no saturation point in education in the whole computer area.

Since the computer industry is comparatively new, we

have not yet had much experience with women who combine the careers of housewife and professional woman. Quite a few of our women workers are married, but the majority are recently married. They generally leave when they become pregnant. Some of these women who are at home with small children are doing part-time programming for computer manufacturers or for other companies. This is an area that may grow in the future.

When some of those married women return to work, perhaps on a full-time basis a little later, there will be some problems. The technology of computers is changing rapidly, like science and engineering technology. Therefore, if a woman stays away for five or six years, she will certainly find her knowledge out of date. But women who have the basic aptitude for this work may be able to come back and learn the new computers. There are also ways in which a woman can try to keep up to date while at home, for example, by reading magazines and journals on the subject. Many programmed textbooks and self-study books are being written about computers and programming languages, and these would certainly help one to keep up to date at least to a limited extent.

In summary, I should like to say that I agree wholeheartedly with Dr. Bettelheim's statement that any woman's most important commitment is to being a woman. In the computer world, normally thought of as a masculine field, the successful women in it have certainly remained feminine. But this has not prevented them from doing their job.

As far as the future is concerned, I do not know what the opportunities for women will be in computers. Time will tell. But I sincerely believe that women have already made a significant contribution in this area, and I feel certain they will continue to do so.

VIVIANNE T. NACHMIAS, *Panelist*

I should like to say first how honored I feel at being asked to join this panel, and to share in the enthusiasm that I feel this symposium is generating. Since I am an example of a married scientist in the early stages of both child rearing and scientific work, and since, moreover, I have elected to work at essentially half speed while my family is young, the topic of this panel is of the greatest interest to me personally.

First I should like to comment specifically on a few points made by Dr. Bettelheim in his interesting discussion. While it is true that the situation of all educated women is basically similar, I think that the problems of the woman who is an experimental scientist differ in at least two important respects from those of other professional women. All fields change and move, of course, but probably the rate of change of scientific and engineering fields is greater than that of some others, for example, perhaps, the humanities. Hence, a prospective researcher or teacher in science can fall behind more drastically in a few years than would a student of some other fields. This makes the return to science after some years of other occupation quite difficult. Second, unlike the artist or writer who needs "a room of one's own" as Virginia Woolf has called it in her marvelous little book, the scientist needs "a lab of one's own" or at least a part thereof, and near to her house, as Miss McCabe has pointed out. Clearly, the one is more readily obtained and equipped than the other. The fact is that the experimental scientist or engineer must, with rare exceptions, go outside the home for work.

Both these points are practical and are obvious to anyone who has thought about the problem a little. However, it is the practical points that are of dominant interest in the life of the working mother who knows roughly what she wants to accomplish. Until she gets to this point, however, the philosophical issues may be more important and of more concern to her.

Dr. Bettelheim has touched upon a number of different attitudes toward the issues of whether woman who are mothers are in a totally unique situation, and whether or how they should attempt to work or have careers. I shall comment here on only one part of this discussion, a part with which I find myself in some disagreement.

Dr. Bettelheim refers to the work of Dr. Erikson, as summarized in *Daedalus* (Spring issue, 1964). I have read the summary of these interesting experiments and find that I am not sure of their relevance to the problem at hand this morning. Dr. Erikson showed, if I understand his summary correctly, that, in free constructions by children under teen age, more than two-thirds of the girls built interiors and were concerned with peaceful and static environments, whereas more than two-thirds of the boys built exterior structures and towers and were concerned more with movement, creation, and destruction. I should like to ask if these experiments really tell us about the essence of women? Or are the results a comment on the essence of our society? Do they tell us how to advise ourselves or other women about careers in science or attitudes toward science?

I should like to make two points. First, what of the other 15 to 25 per cent of girls and boys? For surely not even 20 per cent of girls graduating from college elect to continue as scientists.

Second, how should we interpret the results as they stand?

Should we perhaps conclude that women might be set to work on the interior of the atom — but not on a subject like the emission of radioactivity? Then perhaps Marie Curie might not have made her discoveries. Or should we tell men not to interest themselves in the factors that make for harmony, love, and peace within the family? Then we would not have Erich Fromm to inspire us, perhaps.

I do not mean to detract from the inherent interest of these or similar experiments, but I am arguing that they are not really relevant to our problem, for the very reason that Dr. Bettelheim has stressed. This reason is that, thanks to our wealth, our society can now begin to think about jobs much more in terms of how individual people can and want to work. Especially in fields requiring training and skill, the emphasis can be much more on the individual. Whether it will be depends in part on whether there is a willingness to experiment, as Dr. Bunting has pointed out.

I think it is of the greatest importance that individuals do not feel that, because they are not the norm, therefore they are peculiar in some way. As you can see, I am arguing that the majority of girls may never want to be scientists, but that those who do so choose are sometimes made to feel odd, rather than happy, about their decision, and this is wrong.

This brings me to the central point of this panel — the commitment required — how useful the passive voice. For our society appears to require of a student about to enter a new phase of scholarly life only that he or she have successfully completed the previous phase. With rare exceptions, even scholarship committees do not call back the errant one if he or she decides later, let us say, to become a beatnik. Hence the commitment is largely a personal matter. It may be a commitment to the future. As a woman scientist of my acquaintance put it, "a commitment to the unfinished problem." Or it may derive rather from a sense of what is owed to past opportunities or to people that have helped one, or to the memory of the keen intellectual pleasure that comes from moments of enlightenment or occasional discovery. (For men the commitment usually has an economic basis as well; this aspect varies widely for women.)

However it is derived, the commitment required of a woman entering science today is, I believe, no different in kind from that required of a man; i.e., a serious interest in the subject, a willingness to undertake the necessary training for its study, and a desire to contribute to its continuation and development. The contribution that will arise from this commitment will of course vary with the woman's ability, luck, persistence, preparation, and with her other interests, just as it will with men.

Men, after all, are not so homogeneous a lot, except when one is comparing them with a crowd of women. From my observations, men vary a great deal in their attitude toward science, method of approach, and even in the readiness with which they draw conclusions! Men may be bachelors who spend 60 to 70 hours a week at the laboratory; they may be directors of large research groups, or they may be primarily teachers who conduct research occasionally in the summers. I have even encountered men who do research for enjoyment after regular working hours.

A woman committed to science, who marries and has children, must necessarily work at a slower speed during that time than do most men if she wishes to spend much time with her children. But this does not mean that she does not take science seriously.

Perhaps at this point I should pause and point out that,

since women statistically live longer, perhaps this time is eventually made up.

Dr. Bettelheim has pointed out that the time has come when we can take our work at a more leisurely pace. Perhaps the time will come when we really will be able to. Unfortunately, the working world of science is not geared or paced to half- or part-time positions, by and large. I think this may account for a good deal of wasted talent. There is really no a priori reason why 20 or 50 hours a week is the optimal time for science, and I think a variety of experiments providing opportunities for part-time work are essential. I agree here heartily with Dr. Bunting's remarks. However, anyone working in any discipline does need pieces of time in blocks, and therefore a mother does need help with child care when her children are small. It would be most interesting if universities were to experiment along these lines, perhaps coupling really good child care with an opportunity for students of child psychology to have access to children for observation.

Finally, a commitment to science, as to any discipline, means that a woman takes her interests and potentials seriously, and that she considers them as much a part of her person, to be recognized and developed, as the ability to care for and love her family and other people.

It is, I think, an ironic paradox that this appears to be a psychological problem for many women now, when for the first time in history many more women than ever before are free to have and develop their interests. Perhaps we need a return from the tendency to think of the ideal woman as an ever-young Hollywood sex queen in an ideal house, with ideal children and an ideal husband, to more ancient and more exciting images.

For example, surely, we have not forgotten those visions that Greece has given us: Athena, the winged goddess of wisdom; Diana, the huntress; Circe, the sorceress; and last but not least, Pandora, who was not so very ideal, but was very curious, and wondered what in the world would happen if she just raised the lid a little.

MINA REES, *Panelist*

Like Dr. Bunting, I am anxious to encourage women to enter a profession and, particularly, in view of the shortage that Miss McCabe referred to, the profession of mathematics. I should expect that they would be most welcome. I agree that there are difficulties, and it is undoubtedly true that not a great many women have achieved real distinction in mathematics. But there is no reason to assume that they cannot do it — merely that they have not done it. However, in the graduate school over which I preside, there are now more women than men students in the Ph.D. program in mathematics, and I am glad to report that we are able to give them some financial aid for babysitting. We have not made a kindergarten available to them, although I think that would be more in line with Dr. Bettelheim's suggestion.

I address most of my comments to points that were suggested by Dr. Bettelheim's paper. I am fully in accord with him that "we must start with the realization that, as much as women want to be good scientists and engineers, they want first and foremost to be womanly companions of men and to be mothers." Though we must keep in mind that there is room for the professional woman as well as the professional man who is not married, and that her problems are somewhat different from those of her married sisters, I focus most of my attention on the woman who does marry and thus adds new dimensions to the enrichment of her life and to her fulfillment as a woman.

Married women have a dual job if they are engaged in professional work. For them the time and energy required to achieve excellence in homemaking and raising children can be greatly reduced, but the maximum reduction requires organized social action as well as individual effort. By all means, let us press tirelessly for the social action that Dr. Bettelheim suggests, but let us recognize that the creation of child-care centers where a scientist can leave her child with confidence is only a vision for most places, and that the adjustment of working hours and place of work has been achieved only in a few instances. For the purposes of our discussion today, I prefer to restate the question: " In terms of the expectation of our present society, what are the commitments of a woman entering a scientific profession?"

My comments will deal with three phases of such a woman's commitments — to her professional activities, to her home, and to herself.

First, then, let us consider her commitments to her professional activities. Dr. Bettelheim points out that we must remember that men and women are different. Though I would enthusiastically proclaim, "Vive la différence!" I would add that we must not lose sight of the fact that men and women are also the same. One of my favorite statements on this subject is from a book by George N. Shuster, former president of Hunter College, who said, "Some few things I have found out. One is that you ought not educate a woman as if she were a man, or to educate her as if she were not."

In her professional activities, a woman must operate honestly within the framework of her job. When it comes to technical or scientific or administrative matters, sex differences are irrelevant. If women are to operate on the basis of equality with men, then they must bring to the task the competence and objectivity that the task requires. The way a woman states a case may have feminine components, but the case must meet the issues head on. The feminine quality may be appropriate to the periphery of a professional woman's undertaking, but it is not appropriate to the core.

When I was working in the Office of Naval Research, there was always an interesting question, and a corresponding hesitation, as to whether the Admiral or I would go through the door first. And naval officers were somewhat more tolerant of my impatience with red tape and with hierarchical structure than they were of similar impatience on the part of my male civilian colleagues. But this tolerance in no sense decreased their expectation that, on professional issues, I would ask no quarter nor give any. This is equally true in my present position, where the whole range of academia — including professors, deans, and presidents, as well as registrars and business officers — expects the same kind of professional dealing with me that they have with a man. Other members of our panel are more competent than I to deal with a woman's performance in the laboratory. Dr. Nachmias has already done so. But my own experience would indicate that, first and foremost, a professional woman must be competent in her profession. Her commitments, as she enters a scientific career and during whatever time she continues in it, are the same as those of a man. It is the same whether she marries or not. She is committed to advance knowledge in her field and to safeguard and transmit what is known. She is committed to the search for truth. As Loren Eiseley wrote recently, "Interest, motivation, whatever it is that sets the individual passionately at work is necessary for success." This is as true of a woman as it is of a man. An adverse judgment of her peers on her achievement will not be softened because she is a woman. Nor should her honors and rewards and satisfactions be lessened, but here the tale may be somewhat different.

What of the woman whose professional life is interrupted by her days as homemaker, wife, and mother, when her role, deeply satisfying in its fulfillment, is adjunct to that of her husband and their children? What of the third period of her life when she wishes to enter or re-enter active professional work, possibly continuing her education so that she can do so fully equipped? I am sure that some of the young women who entered M.I.T. have dropped out to follow a career of marriage.

Increasingly, colleges and universities are recognizing their obligation to provide opportunities, during the years of child raising, for continuing intellectual alertness for the women who live in their vicinity, and to stretch their requirements to welcome back to the campus women who did much of their academic work at another institution or whose credits are time worn and need rejuvenation. Both of the preceding speakers mentioned the need for women to remain alert during the years when they are out of their professional work. Increasingly, too, there are programs like the one instituted at Radcliffe by Dr. Bunting, to enable women who have advanced degrees or advanced abilities to re-enter their professions. For each woman, however, there must be the commitment to maintain the currency of her competence in whatever ways are available to her so that, as Dr. Bunting once said to me, "she can come out running" when she is ready to return to professional work. Though others can provide opportunities, each woman must find for herself the means that will enable her to carry on her professional life. And even if we achieve the desirable social organizations and social attitudes that Dr. Bettelheim recommends, a mother must be prepared to give up her work in an emergency — and it may be for weeks or for years. These commitments most women would not wish to evade.

So much for a woman's commitment to her professional life. What of her commitment to her home? I shall say no more about the problems of child raising, since other panelists are better equipped than I am to speak on this question. But for a successful home life, I would say that the most important requirement is to choose the right husband. There is in my mind no doubt of the great advantage many couples have found in having a real community of professional interest. In the professions, as in other walks of life, we are more comfortable with people who speak our jargon. Mathematicians speak to mathematicians, and lawyers to lawyers; but I must add that I find it very attractive indeed to be married to a physician, in spite of George Sarton's observation that "the mathematical and the medical minds are, if not antagonistic, at least very different and sometimes poles apart." Certainly my own experience would indicate that an intellectual woman will look for intellectual companionship and stimulation from her husband, whether their common interests are professional or not. But, granted the choice of the right husband, what of the woman's commitment to her home? I think we must recognize that it will demand a high order of talent and intelligence and attention to make our home life companionable and relaxed, and to make it meet the social demands of both husband and wife. It may be necessary to assign a disproportionate part of your income to full-time help; or it may be possible, by careful choice of professional work, by extraordinarily good management, or by some of the devices mentioned by Dr. Bettelheim, to find the time needed to make a successful home.

I have a friend, one of the most distinguished women mathematicians in the world, who consistently refuses to take a full-time job, and who has worked out, with her mathematician husband, a happy, effective and satisfying marriage. In any case, the commitment of a professional woman, or, for that matter, of a professional man, must include a recognition of the need to cherish and support, and must fulfill the needs for companionship and for the broad enrichment of life in marriage.

Last, what of the commitment of the professional woman to herself? As Dr. Bettelheim says, this is the key question. It is often difficult to know where fulfillment lies, and often we must make disturbing compromises. It may well be that few women have the competitive drive that many men have, and that few women will wish to sacrifice their personal lives to their careers. Always, in considering a new professional opportunity, a married woman will wish to consider its impact not only on her career and on her personal fulfillment, but on her husband as well. Usually her mobility will be limited by his commitments, and she will sometimes find herself unable to achieve the professional recognition that her abilities may merit. In the academic world, those institutions that have been willing to appoint women as professors have often added luster to their faculty that would otherwise have been unattainable, because of the relative lack of mobility of women. This is a fact of life that women, as well as men, accept without much ado. But even when mobility is possible, a woman's commitment to herself as well as to her husband will make her wish to explore as deeply as she can the effect of her career decisions on his happiness and comfort. Hopefully, in most cases, a man will have the same kind of concern for his wife's wishes. Probably this is a problem in which both the similarities and the differences between men and women show themselves most clearly.

Finally, although I would agree with Dr. Bettelheim that women may wisely choose to work less than the demanding workday that usually characterizes our social structure— and that men might well do likewise—I would observe that the top jobs, for men and women alike, are excessively demanding.

If you consider the demands on the time of a man like Dr. Stratton, for example, you may ask whether any women are called upon for such commitments. I believe the answer is that they are, if they undertake positions of top responsibility. And a woman would be well advised to weigh carefully her decision to accept such a demanding position. It may be that a professional married woman has an advantage over her masculine counterpart, because the nature of her concern for her family forces her to give weight to the need for balance and proportion in her commitments outside and inside the home. She is less apt to be trapped into an undertaking that loses sight of her fulfillment as a person in the drive for professional achievement.

I close with a little poem that is perhaps slightly irrelevant, from a new book by Ogden Nash on the pleasures and perils of marriage. Although he addresses it to men, I believe it is equally applicable to women. Here is the little poem:

"To keep your marriage brimming,
With love in the loving cup,
Whenever you're wrong admit it!
Whenever you're right, shut up.[1]

Dorothy M. Simon, *Panelist*

The last time I spoke at M.I.T. my lecture was entitled, "On the Mechanism of Flame Propagation," and I must preface my talk by admitting that I am much better qualified to speak on that subject than on the subject of women in science.

First I should like to expand on one of Dr. Bunting's opening remarks, "To date this country has . . . proceeded on the theory that one does not really expect any significant contribution from women in science."

It appears that not all other countries are proceeding on this hypothesis. Today I want to tell you of some evidence that has come to my attention on this point. In June 1964 the First International Conference of Women Engineers and Scientists was held in New York City under the auspices of the American Society of Women Engineers. My contribution to the conference was to serve as chairman of the Committee for International Travel Grants. Each applicant completed a typical questionnaire, which included biographical and professional career information and a statement of why she wished to attend the conference. One hundred applicants from 15 countries completed the form. These

[1] From *Marriage Lines*. Copyright © 1962 by Ogden Nash. By permission of Little, Brown and Co.

countries represented every continent. Of significance was the ranking of the countries by number of applicants. Tied for first place were the United Kingdom and India with 23 applicants each. Japan was third with eight. It is not surprising to me that the United Kingdom was first, but it is very surprising that the number of applicants from India equaled the number from the United Kingdom.

During the year that I spent as a postdoctoral student at Cambridge University in England it became evident to me that, once a student started graduate work and had definitely made up her mind to become a scientist, the faculty, her colleagues, and other graduate students accepted this fact and proceeded on the theory that she was expected to make a contribution to science. Women in England hold high positions in science and technology, and they have received recognition for their scientific achievements.

The Indian applicants in general held advanced degrees, mostly from universities of prestige in the United Kingdom and the United States. In many cases their graduate study was subsidized by their government. Some of the women had published papers and written chapters of technical books. All were professionally employed. Some were married and many of them had children.

The eight Japanese women were outstanding for their contributions to their field of interest. Two were exceptional because of the large number of papers they had published. One of these women worked in the field of radio chemistry and the other in the field of petroleum chemistry.

Why did all these women want to come to the conference in the United States? Most of them wanted to find out how women in science and engineering were recognized in other countries of the world. In particular, they were very curious about the status of women in the United States. I am sorry to report that these foreign scientists and engineers, after their week in the United States, were not impressed with our status or our leadership in finding ways to contribute to our professions and to be recognized. I often heard the comment from foreign delegates that they were surprised that in the "land of the free" women scientists and engineers had not made more advancement. In fact, my opinion is that, if these women had not been guests in the United States, they would have expressed the thought more strongly by saying that their professional status in their own country, their opportunities for making contributions to science and technology, and their social position were better.

It seems clear that the status of women scientists and engineers is higher in other countries than in the United States, and that the rate of advancement of women is much slower in the United States than in the East. The evidence indicates that it is time in this country to reexamine the hypothesis that women cannot be expected to make significant contributions to science and engineering.

The second point that I would like you to consider as you plan your career is the increased opportunities for scientists in this country. So much has been said and written about new opportunities in the field of research and development and the tremendous growth of applied research that I know you are aware of these changes. But there is another expanding horizon for scientists of which you may not be aware. This is the solution of problems that arise because of scientific discoveries. In the time since the end of the Second World War increasing numbers of scientists have recognized their responsibility to help solve these problems, and in turn they have been called upon by the government and by industry to do so. Positions such as Scientific Advisors to the President of the United States, to congressional committees, to governors, to mayors are all new. Interdisciplinary groups of people including lawyers, statesmen, politicians, sociologists, and scientists are trying to find solutions for the many problems arising from new scientific discoveries — from new curricula for grade-school children to problems affecting the national defense. Scientists and engineers are recognizing that it is their duty to help manage the scientific age. Positions from part-time members of school boards to full-time high-level government positions are becoming available to those who have scientific and engineering training. I suggest that, as you look forward to your own careers in science and engineering, you take into account this new kind of opportunity and see how it can fit your own plans for the future.

In conclusion, I should like to share with you the one most important thing that I have learned in the course of my own career, which is: things are changing. Science and technology go forward at a rapid pace and the forces that bring opportunities in these fields also change in magnitude and direction. It will be necessary for you to be attuned to these changes and to adapt your career to them.

Chien-Shiung Wu, *Panelist*

In his welcoming address, Dr. Stratton, quoting what the generous endower, Matthew Vassar, had said about women's education more than a hundred years ago, said that women have received from the Creator the same intellectual constitution as men and that they should have the same rights and responsibilities as men to add to the scientific and cultural progress of the world. This was the philosophy of the founders of women's education in this country more than a century ago. I am sorry to say that we have made relatively little progress since then. What has contributed to this lack of progress?

I sincerely doubt that any open-minded person really believes in the faulty notion that women have no intellectual capacity for science and technology. Nor do I believe that social and economic factors are the actual obstacles that prevent women's participation in the scientific and technical field. The main stumbling block in the way of any progress is and always has been unimpeachable tradition. It is a "tradition" that the scientific and technical fields have always been men's fields. And, therefore, it is unfeminine for a woman to try to compete with men in a presumably man's field.

Even in his brilliant keynote speech Professor Bettelheim could not refrain from saying that a woman is a woman. He enthusiastically cited the success story of a young Russian girl who worked in the engineering field, but he reminded us that the young Russian girl loved her work with a *womanly embracing* of her tasks rather than a *masculine conquering* of them. He quoted what Balzac said about a woman who has the advantages of a *man's* education. Bringing a womanly point of view may be advantageous in some areas of education and social sciences, but not in physical and mathematical sciences where we strive always for objectivity. I wonder whether the tiny atoms and nuclei or the mathematical symbols or the DNA molecules have any preference for either masculine or feminine treatment.

In science and technology we dedicate ourselves to the study of nature, to the understanding of our environment, and incidentally to the betterment of our life. It is the highest form of aspiration as well as satisfaction. It is a fulfillment of human passion. If, in this human society, women are endowed with just as much intellectual capability as men, why then should they be deprived of such aspiration and fulfillment? Why should they not share the responsibilities (and the satisfactions) of the progress of science with men?

Of course, the qualifications of a scientist are very exacting and the task is demanding, and no one becomes a scientist after a snappy decision and hasty training. It takes long years of study and preparation to become one. If a person had neither the temperament nor the talent or lacked interest in science, he would have been discouraged and dissuaded and would have dropped out long before he was ready for the profession. How unfair it is to shut the door on those women who have met the challenge and come out with flying colors just because they are women!

I believe that the woman's commitment in science and technology is natural, healthy, and promising. It is good for the qualified individuals, and it is *essential* for the future of the country. In a time when we cry for the lack of manpower in science and technology, we find that women's enrollment in science remains low and women employed in the field of science are still few. People are reluctant to face the fact that the lack of women in science is also a terrible waste of potential talent. At this point, may I proudly present some facts to substantiate my claims. I am very proud of women's achievements in nuclear physics. It was the discovery of radioactivity by Professor and Madame Curie that made people realize the existence of the nucleus. Madame Curie discovered and identified several chemical elements and received not one but two Nobel prizes, the first time in physics and the second time in chemistry. No man in history has yet equaled that honor and distinction. Her elder daughter, Madame Irène Curie Joliot, and her husband were also awarded a Nobel Prize for their discovery of artificial radioactivity. We are extremely proud of Dr. Lise Meitner's achievements. She contributed greatly to our understanding of the alpha and gamma radiations. She worked very closely with Dr. Otto Hahn on uranium fission until circumstances forced her to leave Germany. She and her nephew, Dr. Frisch, gave the first explanation of what Hahn had observed and named the process of "nuclear fission," a word borrowed from biology. In 1963 another woman physicist, Dr. Maria Mayer, was awarded the Nobel Prize in physics for her important contribution to the nuclear shell model. Never before have so few contributed so much under such trying circumstances! Why should we not encourage more girls to go to science?

In order to stimulate and encourage women's commitment to science and technology, some fundamental improvements and changes in our attitudes toward women in science must be stressed. One is that we must recognize that the traditional roles of wife and mother and the role of dedicated scientist are actually compatible. The other is the professional acceptance of women scientists and engineers. Professor Bettelheim pointed out that, as much as women want to be good scientists or engineers, they want first and foremost to be womanly companions of men and to be mothers. How can we agree with him any less than wholeheartedly? However, this noble human desire to be devoted companions and good parents must, ideally, be equally shared by men. The social scientists and psychiatrists tell us that the most balanced and normal bringing up of children is under the parental care of *both* father and mother. They also stress the importance of good peer-group relations. In our present society of plenty and proficiency, is it too much to provide excellent professional child care during the day so that mothers can get away from monotonous household chores and work in their chosen field? Is it not more satisfying for a woman to have her own intellectual endeavor along with the responsibility of home and children? Is it not clear that parents who lead more meaningful lives themselves make the time they spend with their children more meaningful for both child and parents?

As for the professional acceptance of women scientists and engineers, the statistics do not speak very favorably for the past or the present. In a report published by the AAUW *Journal* in 1962, John B. Parrish of the University of Illinois compiled special statistics on "Women in Top Level Teaching and Research." The survey was based on the faculty members in ten leading high-endowment and ten leading high-enrollment universities. He showed that women make up about 10 per cent of the faculties. However, women tend to be concentrated in the lower ranks. In the survey, 16 per cent of the instructors, 10 per cent of the assistant and associate professors, but only 5 per cent of the professors were women. Actually, in the physical, biological, and social sciences only 1 per cent of professors are women. The underutilization of women in top-level teaching and research in leading schools is thus severe. However, there seems to be a glimmer of hope on the horizon. Women are currently making substantial contributions at the lower ranks in virtually all fields. There is a good chance that these women are today providing a solid base for the greater (and surely necessary) use of women at the highest levels tomorrow.

PART II

Who Wants Women in the Scientific Professions?

BARRIERS TO THE CAREER CHOICE OF ENGINEERING, MEDICINE, OR SCIENCE AMONG AMERICAN WOMEN

ALICE S. ROSSI

ENHANCING THE ROLE OF WOMEN IN SCIENCE, ENGINEERING, AND THE SOCIAL SCIENCES

JAMES R. KILLIAN, JR.

THE PRESENT SITUATION OF WOMEN SCIENTISTS AND ENGINEERS IN INDUSTRY AND GOVERNMENT

RICHARD H. BOLT

THE PRESENT SITUATION IN THE ACADEMIC WORLD OF WOMEN TRAINED IN ENGINEERING

JESSIE BERNARD

*BARRIERS TO THE CAREER CHOICE OF ENGINEERING, MEDICINE, OR SCIENCE AMONG AMERICAN WOMEN**

ALICE S. ROSSI

Introduction

There is one implication of the topic of the barriers to the career choice of engineering, medicine, or science among

* Grateful acknowledgement is made to the following persons and organizations for support and assistance in the preparation of this paper: to the Carnegie Corporation of New York which supported a bibliographic review of the influences on women's occupational choice, on which this paper draws heavily; to Mrs. Barbara Laslett who assisted me in this review; to the National Institutes of Health, sponsor of my work under a Research Career Development Award (USPHS-K3MH-2376801) as well as current sponsor of the 1961 College Graduate Study at the National Opinion Research Center (MH-05615) from which data are reported herein.

American women on which there appears to be wide agreement, namely, the desirability, for both women and the larger society, of a much greater proportion of women in these fields. But though we agree with this assumption, our reasons for doing so probably differ widely among us. Women students with the intellectual itch to explore and probe some scientific unknown would be grateful if more women were in their student groups and they did not feel, as they often do, that they are viewed as social oddities because of their career choice, and that they run the risk of restricted opportunities for comfortable social relationships with other men and women. Women scientists, engineers, and doctors often wish there were more women in their fields so that in their jobs they did not feel responsible for their whole sex, but just for their own individual performance regardless of their sex. Many policy makers in education and government agree with the assumption for quite different reasons: womanpower is seen as a major reservoir from which the nation may draw to meet the continuing critical shortages in these important professions.

Cutting across and differentiating between men and women among students, government officials, educators, researchers, and the scientists, doctors, and engineers themselves, is considerable variation in the degree to which there is any ideological commitment to the "cause" of women's rights, or the general conviction that more women should play a more involved and significant role in the higher reaches of the occupational system.

In other words, the reasons for accepting the view that more women should enter science, engineering, and medicine may flow from concern with (1) individual personal satisfaction and (2) the enlargement of the minority women represent in these fields and national interest in manpower utilization to (3) a radical transformation of the relations between the sexes as part of an ideology of sex equality.

In my own view, all three reasons are of equal importance. Furthermore, in the paper to follow, my intent is to be provocative, and to insist that many areas of seeming peripheral significance are actually at the root of our topic. Let me start therefore with a few of the propositions I shall make and examine, so that you may know, in advance of the analysis, what certain of my conclusions and convictions are.

> Men believe, and women accept their belief, that woman's role should be selfless, dedicated to being man's helpmeet, and any work or career on the part of women should fill in the gaps of time and energy left over from their primary obligations as wives and mothers. This adaptive role is compatible with a job as a laboratory assistant, engineering aide, or medical technician, but not with responsible careers as scientist, engineer, or doctor, except for those rare Amazons among us who can live two lifetimes in one.

> Part-time employment is this generation's false panacea for avoiding a more basic change in the relations between men and women, a means whereby, with practically no change in the man's role and minimal change in the woman's, she can continue the same wife and mother she has been in the past, with a minor appendage to these roles as an intermittent part-time professional or clerical worker.

> Campaigns to increase the support and encouragement given to the *college-age* woman to enter the

sciences, engineering, or medicine can only effectively reach and help the young woman who is already interested and prepared by a background in science and mathematics to take advantage of opportunities offered her in college. Such women are a tiny minority of their sex, whose experiences at much earlier ages have set in motion an abiding interest in things generally disapproved of for girls in our society. College freshmen do not shift from fine arts to chemistry, or from journalism to engineering, except in rare instances. Hence efforts to be really effective must concentrate on much earlier stages of life and must involve fundamental changes in the rearing of girls and boys.

Studies and observations show that the contemporary college woman persists in wanting a mate more intelligent than herself whom she can "look up to" and thus vicariously experience life and work in his shadow. This is a natural consequence of childhood tears, coquetry, "good" behavior, and dependence on close interpersonal ties. Beneath her jeans and plaid shirt, the girl within has not changed very much from her grandmother in crinoline and lace. Unless enough women want as a mate an intellectual peer and a tender comrade in life and work, few will aspire to or persist in the more demanding professions, and fewer still will make notable contributions to their fields.

I should like to make two general points before outlining the topics to be covered in this paper. For one thing, although pointed attention will be given to the particular fields of the natural sciences, engineering, and medicine, the analysis applies equally well to many other demanding professions in which women are poorly represented — law, architecture, social science, business management. My second point concerns not only why there are so few American women in these fields, but what can be done about it — what strategies can be employed to increase the proportion of women in these fields, at various levels relevant to the problem: the individual woman herself, her parents, her educators, her husband, her government, and her employers. This is not to suggest that proposals for social action will be the major focus, but only that the analysis of the barriers to the career choice of a demanding profession which face American women will, wherever possible, give some attention to what can be done about the situation.

The paper will attempt the following specific things: (1) a brief overview of women's positions in these fields now, and how they have changed in recent years; (2) a preliminary report of the results of a study of women college graduates, summarizing some of the factors that differentiate women who have chosen career fields that are now predominantly chosen by men from those who have chosen careers of a more traditionally feminine nature and from those who see no career field other than homemaking in their future. (3) I shall also attempt a brief profile of how the broad spectrum of career fields differ in the occupational values associated with their choice, with particular attention to the most salient characteristics of the scientist, and what they imply for an interpretation of why women seldom choose scientific careers, or why women have difficulty implementing a choice of a scientific career. I shall conclude with one last report of results from the college graduate study, on the kinds of success women admire in other women, and the kind of success they would like to have themselves.

The Present Pattern of Women's Participation in Science and Engineering

Not many years ago it was possible for a researcher to use U.S. Census data for a great many years after their publication, with the confidence that the basic pattern they showed remained relatively stable. Although this is only 1964, the 1960 census data published in 1961 and 1962 are quickly becoming out of date. When one reads that the total national expenditure on research and development rose from $14.7 billion in 1961–62 to $16.4 billion in 1962–63,[1] only one year later, that the number of engineers and scientists working on NASA programs grew from 8,400 in 1960 to 43,000 in 1963,[2] or that the number of scientists and engineers has grown from 1.3 million in 1960 to 1.4 million in 1963,[3] with an estimate that national requirements for scientists and engineers may be close to 2 million by 1970[4] — one gets a sense that in no segment of the occupational system do census data get out of date more quickly than in the scientific and engineering fields we are concerned with. Nevertheless, these data at least permit a comparative overview of where women stood in these fields in 1960, compared to other fields, and compared to their position ten years earlier.

[1] *National Trends in R & D Funds, 1953–62*, Reviews of Data on Research and Development, No. 41, National Science Foundation, September 1963; and *A Report on Manpower Requirements, Resources, Utilization and Training*, Department of Labor, March 1964, p. 172.

[2] A *Report on Manpower Requirements*, *ibid.*, p. 174.

[3] *Scientists, Engineers, and Technicians in the 1960's, Requirements and Supply*, National Science Foundation, 1964; and *Profiles in Manpower in Science and Technology*, National Science Foundation, 1963.

[4] The expansion in the number of scientists was just as dramatic before 1950: in 1940, the number was 445,000, which grew to 790,000 by 1950, nearly 1.3 million in 1960. Cf. *Profiles in Manpower*, *ibid.*

An examination of the 1960 census data on occupations and sex shows that women accounted for 65 per cent of the increase to the labor force between 1950 and 1960.[5] A few occupations have actually changed from predominantly masculine fields to feminine fields; e.g., the percentage of bank tellers who are women has increased from 45 to 69 per cent, of hucksters and peddlers from 14 to 59 per cent (e.g., "Avon Calling"), of teachers outside the elementary, high school, and college levels (adult education, technical and private schools) from 26 to 61 per cent.[6] There has been no such dramatic change among the professional and technical occupations that concern us: here women represent not 65 but 26 per cent of the increase during the decade of the fifties. This means that in many occupations the number of women has risen strikingly over the decade, but the increase of men has been so much greater that the proportion women represent of the total employed in the field has actually declined. The field of mathematics is a good illustration of this: there has been a 210 per cent increase in the number of women, but the number of men in mathematics increased 428 per cent, with the result that the percentage of mathematicians who are women actually declined from 38 in 1950 to 26 per cent in 1960.

[5] In the next decade, a shift is expected in the sex composition of labor-force growth. From the 65 per cent that women constituted of the increase to the labor force between 1950 and 1960, a decline to 43 per cent of total growth between 1960 and 1975 is the present expectation. The reason lies in the very large increase in young people who will enter the labor force in the decade ahead: since women in this age group work only a short time before withdrawing from the labor market, men will comprise more than half the net increase in the labor force. Cf. A *Report on Manpower Requirements, op. cit.*, pp. 36–37.

[6] U.S. Bureau of the Census, *Census of Population: 1960*, Vol. 1, Table 202, pp. 528–533.

Table I presents the details on the percentage who are women in 1950 and in 1960 as well as the per cent increase for each sex, in the number employed in the scientific, professional, and technical occupations that concern us most directly. In 1960, only 7 per cent of the physicians and sur-

TABLE 1 Women Employed in Science, Engineering, Medicine and Technical Occupations, 1950 and 1960

Selected Occupations	Per cent Female 1960	Per cent Female 1950	Per cent Increase 1950 to 1960 Men	Per cent Increase 1950 to 1960 Women	Total Number 1960	Total Number 1950
Natural scientists						
Total	9.9	11.4	30.0	10.4	149,330	116,918
Agricultural scientists	5.2	5.3	27.6	23.3	7,895	6,200
Biological scientists	26.7	29.2	56.6	38.2	13,937	9,215
Chemists	8.6	10.0	13.5	−3.6	83,420	74,637
Geologists and geophysicists ..	2.3	5.6	81.1	−27.3	18,551	10,598
Mathematicians	26.4	38.0	428.1	209.8	7,527	1,691
Physicists	4.2	6.5	92.5	20.2	13,941	7,422
Miscellaneous ..	9.8	15.9	−39.1	−65.1	4,059	7,155
Engineers						
Total	0.8	1.2	64.3	11.0	860,949	526,179
Aeronautical ...	1.6	1.9	193.9	144.1	51,703	17,650
Chemical	0.9	1.9	27.3	−38.4	41,026	32,543
Civil	0.6	1.6	26.2	−54.7	155,173	124,225
Electrical	0.8	1.2	74.3	19.1	183,887	105,887
Industrial	2.1	1.2	139.5	358.8	97,458	40,278
Mechanical	0.3	0.5	40.9	−8.7	158,188	112,440
Metallurgical ..	0.9	2.0	51.0	−25.7	18,459	12,346
Mining	0.3	0.8	−14.3	−61.5	12,084	14,155
Sales	0.3	[a]	129.1	[b]	56,836	24,734
Not elsewhere classified	0.8	2.3	108.7	−31.4	86,135	41,921
Physicians and surgeons	6.8	6.1	18.1	32.0	228,926	192,520

TABLE 1 (Continued)

Selected Occupations	Per cent Female 1960	1950	Per cent Increase 1950 to 1960 Men	Women	Total Number 1960	1950
Technicians						
Medical and dental	62.4	56.7	56.2	98.6	138,162	76,662
Electrical and electronic	4.6	[a]	643.1	[b]	91,463	11,738
Other engineering and physical sciences ..	12.8	18.0	114.7	43.0	183,609	90,995
Not elsewhere classified	23.6	34.1	309.4	144.7	65,723	18,605

[a] Per cent not shown where less than 0.01.
[b] Per cent increase not shown where less than 0.1 or where base is less than 100.
(Source: U.S. Bureau of the Census, *Census of Population: 1960*, Vol. 1, Table 202, pp. 528–533.)

geons employed in the United States were women, as were 10 per cent of the natural scientists, and less than 1 per cent of the engineers. Within the natural sciences there is considerable variation: from a low of 2 per cent of earth scientists and 4 per cent of physicists to a high of 26 per cent of mathematicians and 27 per cent of biological scientists.[7]

Secondly, the pattern noted for mathematicians holds true to some degree in most of these fields, i.e., the number of

[7] The Committee on Federal Employment of the President's Commission on the Status of Women gathered data on the distribution of women compared to men in various fields and civil service grade levels among federal employees. These data show less variation between physical and biological sciences than the census data do, women being only 4 per cent of the federally employed persons in biological sciences, 8 per cent in physical sciences, and 1 per cent in engineering. Cf. The President's Commission on the Status of Women, *Report of the Committee on Federal Employment*, Appendix D, *Grade and Occupational Distribution of Men and Women in White Collar Jobs*, October 1963.

women in various scientific and engineering fields has increased, but at a rate so much lower than that for men that the proportion of women in the fields is lower in 1960 than in 1950. Thus the percentage who are women has declined in engineering from 1.2 to 0.8 per cent, in the sciences from 11 to 9 per cent, among engineering and physical science technicians, from 18 to 12 per cent. In some fields, like chemistry, the earth sciences and chemical, metallurgical, mining, and civil engineering, there are actually fewer women in 1960 than in 1950. This appears to be compensated for in engineering by a marked increase in the number of women in industrial engineering: a 359 per cent increase compared to men's 140 per cent increase, with the result that the percentage who are women in this engineering field has increased from 1.2 to 2.1 per cent. I do not know enough about engineering specialties to interpret this in very specific terms, but the same phenomenon may be at work there that appears in other segments of the labor force: women replace men at lower levels of a broad occupational field as the upper reaches of the field expand and are filled by men.[8] Thus women have been slowly replacing men as bank tellers as men move up into the expanding categories of higher

[8] In an analysis of the position of minorities in the labor force from 1900 to 1960, Dale Hiestand points out that white women have been of diminishing importance in the growth of the professional and related occupations as the over-all growth rates in these fields have accelerated. This occurs because the growth pattern of the majority group (white males) defines the rapidly growing fields; since minorities in the labor force like white women or Negro males and females constitute a small proportion of the total labor force by definition, they can usually provide only a small proportion of the added manpower in rapidly growing fields. Cf. Dale L. Hiestand, *Economic Growth and Employment Opportunities for Minorities*. New York: Columbia University Press, 1964.

status managerial jobs in banking and business corporations.[9] So in many of the jobs included in industrial engineering, women may be filling the vacancies left by men in industrial firms that produce consumer products as these men move into more complex and expanding engineering specialties,[10] such as nuclear engineering.

Education

There is one important fact that complicates an attempt to describe and assess women engineers as compared to men engineers. When we think of an "engineer" we have in mind a much better trained individual than many who informed the census enumerators that they were employed as "engineers." We may have an image of a woman with, at a minimum, a college degree, but only 37 per cent of the 7714 women engineers in the 1960 census have a bachelor's degree or better, in contrast to 56 per cent of the men engineers. In fact, 44 per cent of these women engineers have had no college training of any kind. Even allowing for considerable learning and technical training on the job, it seems highly

[9] There appears to be a trend toward greater sex-linking of jobs in the technician occupations than in the past. Thus the percentage who are women among medical-dental technicians has actually increased from 56 to 62 per cent between 1950 and 1960, while among engineering and physical science technicians the percentage has decreased from 18 to 12 per cent. Cf. Table 1.

[10] It is also of interest that, although there are fewer women employed as chemical engineers in 1960 than in 1950, chemical engineering has continued to be the major field of undergraduate concentration among women engineering students. In the study of undergraduate women in engineering in 1963, as in a study of all women who earned engineering degrees in the past, chemical engineering is the largest field of concentration, but among employed women engineers, more women are in electrical, industrial, and civil engineering than in chemical engineering. Cf. source notes (*b*) and (*c*) to Table 3 in the text.

unlikely that very many of these women engineers without college training are actually doing work that could be classified as professional engineering. Furthermore, as Table 2 shows, the proportion of women engineers with only high

TABLE 2 Educational Attainment of Scientists and Engineers, Experienced Civilian Labor Force, by Sex, 1960 (in per cent)

	Median School Years Completed	High School Graduate or Less	Some College	College Graduate	College Graduate Plus	Base Number
Scientists						
Male	16.8	13	11	32	43	(135,649)
Female	16.5	15	15	40	30	(14,616)
Engineers						
Male	16.2	24	20	38	18	(862,002)
Female	13.9	44	19	25	12	(7,714)
Selected engineering fields among women:						
Aeronautical		31	26	33	10	(778)
Chemical		64	4	9	21	(563)
Civil		22	19	42	17	(721)
Electrical		38	17	31	14	(1,602)
Industrial		60	18	16	6	(2,286)
Mechanical		28	35	27	10	(577)

(Source: U.S. Bureau of the Census, *Census of Population: 1960. Subject Reports. Occupational Characteristics*, Final Report PC(2)-7A, 1963, Table 9.)

school diplomas at most is particularly high in industrial and chemical engineering, where they constitute 60 per cent or more of the categories. Many of these women, then, are more accurately described as technicians, engaged in such things as quality control testing, than as engineers.

This complicates any attempt to compare specialty in employment with specialty in the engineering training that preceded employment. There are some data from the Society

TABLE 3 Engineering Specialities among Employed College Graduate Engineers, Women Engineering Degree Holders, and Women Engineering Undergraduates (in per cent)

	Employed Engineers[a] College Graduates Men	Employed Engineers[a] College Graduates Women	All Women with Engineering Degrees[b]	Women Engineering Undergraduates[c]
Engineering Specialty				
Aeronautical . . .	6	12	7	5
Chemical	7	6	21	20
Civil	18	15	14	9
Electrical	22	25	18	15
Industrial	9	18	3	3
Mechanical	18	8	18	10
Metallurgical, mining	2	4	3	2
General and other, not elsewhere classified	17	12	16	35
N =	(479,819)	(2,830)	(1,582)	(1,014)

[a] U.S. Bureau of the Census, *Census of Population: 1960*. Subject Reports. *Occupational Characteristics*, Final Report PC(2)-7A, 1963, Table 9.
[b] Preliminary Report, *Women Engineering Graduates*, Society of Women Engineers, June 1964 (mimeograph).
[c] *Biennial Survey of Undergraduate Women Engineering Day Students*, Society of Women Engineers, Fall 1963.

of Women Engineers on the fields in which women have earned engineering degrees in the past, and the fields in which women undergraduates in engineering schools were concentrating in 1963. To compare employed women engineers with these samples, and with men engineers, Table 3 confines the employed men and women to those possessing at least a college degree.[11]

The rank order for both women undergraduate students[12] and women degree holders is roughly the same: the first rank is chemical engineering, the second is shared between electrical and mechanical engineering. Very few women have taken degrees or are currently majoring in industrial engineering in engineering schools. Employed women engineers with a college degree are found most frequently in electrical engineering, as are their counterparts among men. But in second place is mechanical engineering for the men and industrial engineering for the women. These data suggest that the specialized training of men "fits" their eventual employment specialty to a greater extent than does that of women.[13] Why this is so I can only guess: the measuring cup for a cooking

[11] This does not necessarily mean an engineering degree; some proportion of these degree holders are presently employed as engineers but took their college degrees in other, though probably related, fields.

[12] This sample is heavily biased by women in their freshmen and sophomore years in engineering schools. Since first-year students often drop out, flunk out, or shift fields, the normal process of attrition will sharply reduce the size of this group by four years hence. It is because of the heavy proportion of entering students that the "other" category is so large: many have not yet decided on a field of concentration.

[13] Stanley Robin's samples of male and female engineering students (junior and senior years) show the following contrast among these specialties:

	Chemical	Civil	Electrical	Industrial	Mechanical	Other	
Men	9	5	33	3	26	19	(76)
Women	29	12	14	8	8	29	(77)

These data are no more than suggestive, however, for the women were drawn from a nation-wide list of undergraduate engineering women, whereas the men represent a random sample of men engineering students at one institution, Purdue University. Cf. Stanley Shane Robin, *A Comparison of Male-Female Roles in Engineering*, Ph.D. dissertation, Purdue University, 1963, p. 60.

recipe, the test tube or microscope in a high school chemistry or biology laboratory, and a subsequent specialization in chemical engineering may be a linked sequence of interests along the life line of the woman. Dismantling an old car, or building a raft and setting up an intercom system with a friend, may be the boyhood experiences that propel the male to high school physics where a course is available,[14] and on to mechanical and electrical engineering. We would have to know a great deal more than we do — about the type of industry and the kind of work women engineers are doing who had majored in chemical engineering but are working as industrial engineers — to know if there is any actual lack of fit between their school training and the jobs they hold.

Income, Type of Employer, and Hours Worked Weekly

It is a simple matter to establish the fact that there is a decided difference between men and women in the income they earn in the scientific and engineering fields, but it is a complex matter to interpret with any satisfaction what accounts for this income difference. It is a fact that the median salary of men is between $2,500 and $3,000 higher than that of women in the scientific fields. One cannot simply conclude, however, that women are underpaid compared to

[14] At the turn of the century physics was taken by more students than any other science. Although the number of high school physics students has increased, the rate has been much lower than for chemistry or biology. At the turn of the century about 20 per cent of the total public high school enrollment was enrolled in physics; this had dropped to under 5 per cent by 1964. Chemistry has remained relatively constant over the half-century, with something under 10 per cent of the high school enrollment taking a chemistry course. Biology has shown the major growth, from under 5 per cent of the students in 1910 to about 25 per cent by 1964. Cf. *Physics: Education, Employment, Financial Support, A Statistical Handbook.* American Institute of Physics, 1964, pp. 2–3.

men, for there are a number of reasons why women cannot be expected to earn as large an income as men. One reason, as we have noted before, is that women do not go on for advanced degrees to the same extent that men in these fields do. There is a steady decline in the percentage who are women in all scientific fields as you move from the bachelor's to the master's and the doctor's degree level, as shown in Table 4.[15]

TABLE 4 Percentage Who Are Women in Selected Scientific Fields, by Degree Earned in 1961–1962

	Bachelor's		Master's		Doctorate	
	Per cent	No.	Per cent	No.	Per cent	No.
Biology	34	(10,018)	29	(804)	15	(178)
Mathematics	29	(14,610)	19	(2,680)	6	(396)
Chemistry	21	(8,086)	17	(1,404)	6	(1,114)
Astronomy	17	(46)	17	(46)	4	(25)
Geology	5	(1,404)	3	(550)	1	(182)
Physics	4	(4,812)	4	(1,425)	2	(667)

(Source: Office of Education data cited in *Physics: Education, Employment, Financial Support, op. cit.*, Appendix B, pp. 80–81.)

However, the fact that there is a higher proportion of advanced degrees in the scientific and technical fields among men than among women does not account for very much of the income discrepancy between men and women. As seen in Table 5, at each level of educational attainment, and in each field, the median salary of men is considerably higher than that of women.

Another source of the income difference between men and

[15] Comparable data from the Office of Education for the distribution of earned degrees during the years 1949–1950 to 1961–1962 show an increase in the proportion who are women only among bachelor's degree holders in biology and chemistry, and master's degree holders in biology.

TABLE 5 Median Salary of Employed Scientists and Engineers, by Sex and Degree, 1962

		Men	Women
Engineering			
	Bachelor's	$10,019	$ 7,576
	Master's	11,033	7,886
	Doctorate	13,635	10,295
Physics			
	Bachelor's	8,549	6,744
	Master's	9,503	6,633
	Doctorate	12,276	8,452
Biology			
	Bachelor's	7,211	5,845
	Master's	7,663	6,324
	Doctorate	9,881	8,291
Mathematics-statistics			
	Bachelor's	8,516	7,160
	Master's	9,220	6,702
	Doctorate	11,404	9,273

(Source: Unpublished data from a post-censal survey of professional and technical occupations, presently under analysis by Seymour Warkov, National Opinion Research Center, University of Chicago.)

women is the type of employer they have. Using data from the 1962 National Register of Scientific and Technical Personnel, Table 6 shows that, although the men and women scientists in this register do not differ markedly in educational attainment,[16] they differ strikingly in the type of employer they have. Almost half the women but only a quarter of the men work in educational institutions; just the reverse holds for industrial and self-employment, where almost half the men, but only a fifth of the women, are located.

[16] The same proportion of women as of men scientists in the 1962 Register hold doctorate degrees (31 per cent). Women scientists more often have master's degrees than men (39 per cent compared to 25 per cent), less often just the bachelor's degree or less educational attainment (27 per cent compared to 40 per cent).

TABLE 6 Type of Employer and Work Activity of Men and Women Scientists (in per cent)

	Men	Women
Type of Employer		
Education	27	48
Government	17	16
Nonprofit	4	8
Industry and self-employed	46	20
Other	4	2
No report	2	6
Work Activity		
Research, development, and design	35	37
Management	24	6
Teaching	15	29
Other	25	23
N =	(200,362)	(14,578)

(Source: 1962 National Register of Scientific and Technical Personnel, cited in *Physics: Education, Employment, Financial Support*, *op. cit.*, Table 32, p. 60.)

This does not mean that half these women are teaching, for many are on research staffs in colleges and universities, as can be seen in the lower half of the table. Since men are four times more likely to be in management than women, and women twice as likely to be teaching as men, here is part of the reason for the income difference between the sexes.[17]

[17] Data from the post-censal survey provide further detail on the contrast between physical and biological sciences. In the physical sciences, women at both the master's and the doctorate level are more apt to be employed by colleges and universities than are men, who are predominantly in business and industry. In contrast, there are no major sex differences at any educational level in the biological sciences. Biologists with relatively low levels of advanced education are more apt to be employed in government and at the higher levels of educational attainment by educational institutions than is the case for physical scientists.

Another difference between the sexes that might explain the contrast in their incomes is the length of the work week. If a large number of women work part time, their annual salaries, even for comparable levels of experience and training, will necessarily be lower than the men's. Actually, as Table 7 shows in detail, there are very few women in part-time employment in either engineering or the natural sciences, unless they are located in educational institutions. In the hard core of the fields — in industrial employment — women are only slightly more apt to work part time than men. A more marked contrast between the sexes is that men work overtime to a much greater extent than women do. The average weekly hours worked are about the same for engineers as for scientists: 42 or 43 hours a week for the men, 39 hours a week for the women. Roughly 10 per cent of the women work less than 35 hours a week compared to 1 per cent of the men. However, only 14 per cent of the women scientists work 41 or more hours a week compared to 27 per cent among the men. Table 7 also suggests that, even if a married woman were willing to take a job as a technician, she has at present little chance of securing a part-time job. The pattern of full-time or overtime work holds as true for the technicians as for the engineers and scientists. If a woman wants to work in engineering or the sciences, the chances are still rather slim that she will find a part-time job unless she wishes to teach her subject.

The work week of professors and instructors in the sciences and engineering is of special interest, for the data show a very wide leeway in the weekly hours they work. Sizable numbers of academic men work even longer weeks than their industrial counterparts — the hard working professor is a reality behind these statistics — but the possibility also exists for relatively short work weeks. Undoubtedly this reflects

TABLE 7 Weekly Hours Worked by Employed Engineers, Scientists, and Technicians, by Sex, 1960

	Mean No. Hours		No. Hours Worked (in per cent)					
	Men	Women	Men			Women		
			1–34	35–40	41+	1–34	35–40	41+
Engineers	42.8	38.6	1	67	32	9	82	9
Scientists	42.1	38.6	5	68	27	11	75	14
Biologists	43.0	39.1	6	58	36	12	66	21
Chemists	41.6	38.8	4	72	24	9	80	11
Mathematicians	41.4	38.6	3	74	23	6	87	7
Physicists	41.6	[a]	5	72	23	18	59	23
Professors-instructors								
Biological sciences	43.6	33.8	17	28	54	37	28	35
Chemistry	40.8	[a]	25	25	50	41	26	33
Engineering	42.5	[a]	15	32	53	60	20	20
Mathematics	36.4	35.4	34	30	36	37	31	32
Physics	40.5	[a]	26	26	48	54	—	46
Technicians								
Medical and dental	42.2	38.5	10	51	39	15	61	24
Electrical and electronic	42.2	39.8	3	70	27	5	81	14
Other engineering and physical science technicians	41.5	38.7	4	71	25	8	80	12

[a] Mean not shown when case base less than 1000.
(Source: U.S. Bureau of the Census, *Census of Population: 1960*. Subject Reports. *Occupational Characteristics,* Final Report PC(2)-7A, 1963, Table 13.)

variation among the men in the extent to which they are involved in research, consultation, and conferences beyond their teaching obligations. As for the women who teach science and engineering, more of them are either on part-time schedules or on overtime schedules than are putting in normal full-time weeks of between 35 and 40 hours. It would be interesting to know whether this pattern differentiates single women from married women in teaching, but no data have been found on this question. In any event, moonlight appears to be confined to romantic association for women, and not to a second job as it is for many men in these occupations.

Nor is this contrast between men and women confined to the technical and scientific occupations. Table 8 brings together the census data on the weekly work patterns of men and women in a selected number of occupations which are traditionally considered "feminine" fields, such as nursing, school teaching, secretarial work. The contrast between the sexes is even sharper in some of these "feminine" fields than

TABLE 8 Weekly Hours Worked by Those Employed in Selected "Feminine" Occupations, by Sex, 1960

	Mean No. Hours		No. Hours Worked (in per cent)					
	Men	Women	Men			Women		
			1–34	35–40	41+	1–34	35–40	41+
Librarians	32.4	32.9	33	51	16	31	58	11
Professional nurses	43.8	37.9	7	57	36	21	57	22
Social welfare workers	41.7	38.3	7	63	30	13	73	14
Teachers, elementary school	42.5	36.5	13	47	40	29	55	17
Teachers, secondary school	44.4	38.2	9	43	48	22	54	23
Secretaries	41.3	37.1	11	52	34	14	75	11

(Source: U.S. Bureau of the Census, *Census of Population: 1960*. Subject Reports. *Occupational Characteristics*, Final Report PC(2)-7A, Table 13.)

it is in the scientific and engineering fields. Men are moonlighting to a considerable extent, particularly in teaching, and though full-time jobs are the general rule even in these feminine occupations, there is a significant minority of women who work less than 35 hours a week.

Marital Status

The last of the topics on which we can describe women engineers and scientists in a broad demographic way is to

TABLE 9 Marital Status of Engineers, Scientists, and Physicians, by Sex, Experienced Civilian Labor Force, 1960 (in per cent)

		Single	Married, Spouse Present	Separated, Divorced, or Widowed	Base No.
Scientists, natural					
	Men	13	84	3	(135,649)
	Women	45	43	12	(14,616)
Engineers					
	Men	9	88	2	(862,002)
	Women	37	45	18	(7,714)
Physicians and surgeons					
	Men	7	88	5	(214,830)
	Women	31	51	18	(15,477)
Professors-instructors					
Natural sciences[a]					
	Men	17	79	4	(31,474)
	Women	56	33	11	(3,911)
Engineering					
	Men	12	86	2	(9,805)
	Women	36	64	—	(221)

[a] Includes agricultural sciences, biological sciences, chemistry, geology, geophysics, mathematics, physics, and natural sciences not elsewhere classified.
(Source: U.S. Bureau of the Census, *Census of Population:* 1960. Subject Reports. *Occupational Characteristics,* Final Report PC(2)-7A, 1963, Table 12.)

examine their marital status compared to men in their fields. Once again, the data are not as adequate as one would like, for Table 9 is based on all the self-reported engineers and scientists in the 1960 Census and therefore includes a large proportion of the pseudo-engineer women with very low educational attainment, as noted earlier. It is a safe assumption that these women are more apt to be married than the women with advanced degrees, and hence the data probably underestimate the proportion of unmarried women among employed engineers who have had professional engineering education.

In all the fields shown in Table 9, women are from three to four times more likely than men to be single. Four out of five men are married and living with their wives, but an average of only two out of five women in engineering, science, or medicine are married and living with their husbands.[18] Data from the post-censal survey of these occupations indicate that educational attainment bears no relationship to marital status among men, but among women the proportion married declines with each degree beyond the bachelor's. These same data indicate that a smaller proportion of

[18] These census data show a much lower proportion married among engineers than do the data on women with engineering degrees collected by the Society of Women Engineers, which showed 80 per cent of the women married. This can be accounted for largely by the fact that their data are based on *all* women with engineering degrees and includes all the many women who married and left employment, whereas the census data are for *employed* women engineers. Of the women with engineering degrees 47 per cent were not employed and the preliminary report does not show the proportion married among those employed. Cf. Preliminary Report, *Women Engineering Graduates*, Society of Women Engineers, June 1964 (mimeograph). Based on their lists of women, I calculated that among those who earned degrees since 1950, 71 per cent of those with bachelor's but 61 per cent of those with master's or doctor's degrees were married.

the younger women in these fields are single than of the older women, whereas there is no age relationship to marital status among the men in these fields.

Whether one takes comfort in this new trend or finds it disturbing depends on who you are. To the single young student, it may represent an encouraging sign that she is less likely to remain unmarried if she pursues her advanced training than were the women of an older generation. To those concerned with whether or not that advanced training will be completed or whether the training will be put to use, the response may be less enthusiastic, for marriage is related to withdrawal from college, graduate school, and employment, so that career choices are less apt to be implemented. This whole question is one so many of us have been concerned with and had conflicts about that it warrants some extended comment.

To begin with, let us examine the differences higher education and advanced degrees make in the lives of women versus men. I think it is generally the case that a man's expectation of what he wants in a wife is essentially unchanged as he moves through his advanced training: whether he is a college junior majoring in biology or an interne in medicine, he may choose the same kind of woman, though his motivation for marriage at 20 probably differs from his motivation at 26. In other words the man's expectation of what he wants in a wife remains relatively stable, regardless of the amount of specialized training he receives.

I think this is very different for a woman. Her expectations of what she wants in a husband are apt to change significantly as she advances in higher education. The man who attracts her when she is a college junior may have no appeal for her when she is matriculated for a Ph.D. This tends to be viewed in terms of higher education's "restricting the woman's chance to marry," which implies an image of the woman merely waiting to be chosen. Consistent with this is the feeling that, if men do not want intellectual career women, then a woman should not become one because fewer men may want her as a wife.

Perhaps it would be better psychologically if women saw the other side of this: as she gains advanced training and confidence in her ability to master an exciting field of study and an important job, she may not want to marry many men she would have had no objection to earlier in her life. She is not an object less desirable in the eyes of men, but a woman who finds fewer men desirable. Since this is so, she may indeed be less apt to marry. On the other hand, if she *does* marry, she may be far more likely to form a satisfying relationship than her less well-trained female friends. There is no research evidence on this, for it involves an assessment of the *quality* of the relationship between spouses. What we do know, however, is that in at least a few fields in which it has been studied, professional women are highly likely to marry men in their own or closely related fields. Thus among married women with professional engineering degrees, 55 per cent had married men who were also engineers or scientists.[19] In another study which contrasts women and men physicians, the same high proportion of the married women doctors had husbands in medicine or related fields.[20]

[19] *Women Engineering Graduates, op. cit.*

[20] R. A. Dykman and J. M. Stalnaker, "Survey of Women Physicians Graduating from Medical School, 1925–1940," *Journal of Medical Education*, 32, part 2, 1957, 3–38. Edgerton did a follow-up study of women who competed for the 1942–43 Westinghouse Science Scholarship Awards. He notes that among the working married women, three out of five had husbands in the same or allied fields and were unanimous in stressing the support their husbands gave in their attempt to complete their advanced training and remain in their fields after

In an era in which early marriage is the pervasive pattern, perhaps the unusually competent professional young woman would do well to remember that a very high proportion of very youthful marriages fail. If she postpones marriage in order to complete her training and secure some professional work experience, the result may be that, when she does marry, it will be to a previously married man who is now mature enough to seek and appreciate the qualities of intellect and shared interests which the professional woman brings to a marriage. I realize that this is a pragmatic view that is not in keeping with the romantic image of the relations between the sexes with which our society is inundated, and it also clashes with the very conservative views regarding sex and marriage that still plague us. But our sexual mores and views of marriage are in a state of considerable flux and change, and I think some of us should begin to think beyond this present chaos to a new set of desiderata for marriage more appropriate to the world we are making, and to reject the burdens of a past if they are no longer adequate to our present stage of societal development. The first steam engine or sewing machine is now a museum piece, but our social patterns often remain the constraints within which we live rather than the part of our history many such patterns should become.

It has often struck me as odd that, despite the importance marriage has in our personal lives — in our anticipation and experience of it — and despite the volumes of research and speculation concerning marriage which educators and social scientists have amassed, we know relatively little about the effect of marriage upon women's values, self-conceptions,

---

marriage. H. A. Edgerton, "Women in Science Careers," *National Association of Women Deans and Counselors*, 25, June 1962, 166–169.

and expectations for their future. Nor do we really know very much about the difference in personality characteristics and emotional needs of couples who marry at very young ages compared with those who marry in their mid or late twenties. High school and college students being a prime captive research group to psychologists and sociologists alike, we do know a bit about what differentiates women who marry under twenty years of age from those who are still unmarried at twenty. One such study started with personality measures administered to girls while in high school and several years later established which young women had married and which were still single. These single and married women were then individually matched for age, intelligence, nationality, birth order, and father's occupation; and their personality tests were examined to determine whether the single and married women differed at all. The results indicated that the single girls were more self-reliant, had a greater sense of personal freedom, showed less tendency to withdraw, were more aggressive socially, and better adjusted emotionally.[21] Research of this sort suggests that women who have married young have done so out of weakness rather than strength, that they had considerable ego-deficiency and were seeking in marriage their "identity in intimacy" as Sanford has described it.[22]

But the tantalizing question that remains unanswered is what effect marriage itself has upon the woman, quite apart from this selective process. What would the results of the personality tests show if they were administered after marriage and compared to the premarriage scores? That marriage

[21] Floyd M. Martinson, "Ego Deficiency as a Factor in Marriage," *American Sociological Review*, 20, April 1955, 161–164.

[22] Nevitt Sanford, "Personality Development during the College Years," *Journal of Social Issues*, 12, No. 4, 1956, 71.

itself has dramatic effects on the lives of women scarcely needs research if our attention is kept to such gross variables as participation in the labor force, amount of schooling completed, interpersonal association, and so forth. But I am concerned with the more subtle psychological variables such as autonomy and submissiveness, and with fundamental values concerning sex role or traditional beliefs. One study conducted at Michigan State University[23] offers some suggestive clues: the top 1 per cent of a freshman class of women were studied periodically during their four years at college, and the researchers found that the women who married before completing their college program actually changed from the personality profile they showed as freshmen: after marriage, they showed less independence, reduced impulse expression, greater submissiveness and conservatism. Other research at MSU has ascertained that men were slightly more traditional and conservative and held to more fundamental values than the women, with the clear implication that the women who married (and 60 per cent of MSU women marry MSU men) changed in the direction of the characteristics of the men they married. They had lost the gains they had made in developing their own particular value system during the middle years of their college careers and were showing the adaptive role in their marital relationship that I discussed earlier.

Women College Graduates, Class of 1961: Marriage and Career Types

My own current research is based on a sample of women college graduates of the class that was graduated in June

[23] Dorothy Robinson Ross, *The Story of the Top 1% of the Women at Michigan State University*, 1963 (mimeograph).

1961. They have been sent four questionnaires during the period from the spring of 1961 when they were college seniors to the summer of 1964 when they had been out of college for three years. One major focus of this research is on career choice and the implementation of career plans, but the women in the sample were also questioned in considerable detail in the 1964 questionnaire concerning their actual experiences in and expectations of their domestic and family roles. At this writing, final results are only now becoming available for detailed analysis, but several preliminary excursions[24] have been made into these data which are of relevance to many aspects of the problem of why so few American women are found in the scientific and top professional fields.

One such excursion was to examine the differences among three types of women, classified by the extremely different career goals they had, as follows:

1. *Homemakers:* These are women who reported in

[24] The data from the most recent questionnaire in this longitudinal study of college graduates only became available for final analysis in the spring of 1965, several months after the first draft of this paper was written. The presymposium version of the paper was therefore based on data from a nonrandom subsample of the first questionnaire returns. Wherever possible this final version of the paper has revised the figures to accord with patterns shown in the final total sample. This does not apply, however, to any figures given in the comparison of pioneers and homemakers, which are exclusively based on the nonrandom subsample. Results are therefore not presented in tabular form unless they stem from the final results of the total sample. There is little reason to expect major shifts in any of the patterns reported, however, since the preliminary analysis was based on 3,500 of the approximately 8,000 women who responded to this wave of the study. For a description of the study and the results from the questionnaires administered before college graduation, cf. James A. Davis, *Great Aspirations.* Chicago: Aldine Publishing Company, 1964.

1964 that they had no career goal other than being "housewives." [25]

2. *Traditionals:* Women whose long-range career goals are in fields in which women predominate: elementary and secondary school teachers (excluding mathematics and science teachers), social workers, nurses, librarians, secretaries, and home economists.

3. *Pioneers:* Women whose long-range career goals are in predominantly masculine fields: the natural sciences, business management, public and educational administration, medicine, law, engineering, dentistry, architecture, economics.

The homemakers represent one-fifth of the sample of these women college graduates, and almost 90 per cent of them are married. The traditionals represent not quite half the women, and about two-thirds of them are married. The pioneers are only 7 per cent of the women, and half of them are married at this point in their lives.

There are interesting differences between single and married women in these three career types. Although the details of this analysis will be presented elsewhere, there is one striking impression that warrants presentation and discussion here. Among the pioneers, marriage appears to have the effect of restricting their expectations concerning the place of work and career in their lives, whereas for homemakers and traditionals, marriage has the effect of restricting their

[25] The question on which the typology is based was: "Which field from the list in the cover letter best describes your anticipated long run career field? If you are a woman: if you plan to combine marriage and work, code the field of employment, not housewife. Use the code number for 'housewife' ONLY if you do not expect to work at all."

expectations concerning the place of family roles in their lives. It is almost as though the pioneers had romantic notions concerning careers and work which the reality of advanced study and employment temper, and homemakers had romantic notions concerning marriage and family roles which the reality of marriage and motherhood tempers.[26]

How does this pattern show itself? The majority of the women (and a sizable proportion of men) expect "family relationships" to be the primary source of satisfaction in their lives, but among the single pioneers a large minority (some 40 per cent) expect "career" to be the primary source of life satisfaction. Less than 10 per cent of the married pioneers share this expectation. That pioneers in some sense expect this to happen is suggested by the fact that two-thirds of both the single and the married pioneers agree with the view that "it is more important for a woman to help her husband's career than to have one herself," implying as this does that marriage leads to putting her own career in second place. The pioneer in no sense regrets the choice of her field, agreeing to a large extent that more women should be encouraged to enter the "masculine" occupations and claiming that they would personally encourage any young woman with the interest and ability to enter such fields. On family-related items, the single and married pioneers do not differ: very few want to have large families, and the majority of both single and married pioneers approve of a woman's taking a part-time job when her child

[26] To simplify presentation of results, I shall exclude the traditional women from most of the discussion, comparing instead just the pioneers and the homemakers. On all the variables discussed, unless otherwise noted, the traditionals fall between the pioneers and the homemakers in their response profile, though much closer in most cases to the homemakers than to the pioneers.

is a preschooler. Of special sociological interest is the further finding that few pioneers express any special enjoyment in "being with young children" or "visiting with relatives."

Marital status makes a decided difference among homemakers on these family-related items. Single homemakers want large families to a significantly greater extent than do married homemakers. (Only 7 per cent of both single and married pioneers want 5 or more children, but 22 per cent of the single homemakers to 10 per cent of the married homemakers want families of this size.) Of even greater interest is the difference between single and married homemakers on the age they believe a child should be before the mother takes a part-time job: only 16 per cent of the single homemakers say "under five years of age," but fully 35 per cent of the married homemakers approve maternal employment when a child is still a preschooler.[27]

[27] The fact that differences of this magnitude differentiate between single and married homemakers should alert the social scientist against putting too much credence in the future expectations of young women when they are in college. One could readily predict far more conservatism concerning maternal employment than actually exists once these women are older and have such responsibilities in the home. One study, which shows perhaps the most conservative attitudes toward working wives of any study I have seen, should perhaps be viewed with this in mind. This study of college freshmen showed that the majority of the men and the women rejected the view that work to fulfill the self is appropriate for married women, though they accepted such employment when it stemmed from selfless motivation on the part of women. Thus they reject the view that women should work in order to have a life of their own and to use their abilities and training, and feel that this is the way women should feel. Yet the majority approve motivation such as "so their husband can complete his education" or to meet financial responsibilities, or to buy things for the home and family. College freshmen are still far enough from the reality of marriage to believe that it will or should fulfill women completely, a view that will be modified as they experience marriage and parenthood. It may also be that a generation of permissive childrearing has produced young

The pattern of response to the activities that these women now "very much enjoy" has several points of interest. Certain things seem to decline in interest as a woman shifts from a single to a married state, while others increase in interest. Single women are more apt than married women to enjoy very much "active sports," "being with male friends," and "art and music" — one gets the image of the dating and courting couple at sports and cultural events. Married women are more apt than single women to enjoy the domestic activities of sewing and cooking. These are all predictably related to marital status. That marital status does *not* relate to "visiting with relatives" and "being with young children" is more surprising. Yet these two items are strongly related to career types: only one-third of both single and married pioneers very much enjoy being with young children, something that two-thirds of both single and married homemakers enjoy. Similarly only one-quarter of the pioneers, as compared to half of the homemakers, enjoy "visiting relatives."

What does this pattern mean? I believe the major part of the answer lies in the different meaning close interpersonal ties have for the homemaker, as compared with the pioneer, and represents part of the source of the very different paths these women are following in their adult lives. Women whose childhood was characterized by intense and extensive relationships with their families, with relatives as well as members of their immediate nuclear family, are far more

---

adult women far less selfless than their mothers and grandmothers, women who feel they should serve their children and husbands but are not psychologically capable of such devotion to others. Cf. Vivian H. Hewer and Gerhard Neubeck, *College Freshmen's Attitudes toward Working Wives,* University of Minnesota Research Bulletin of the Office of the Dean of Students, February 1964 (mimeograph).

apt to grow up with a very conservative image of appropriate roles for women: these are the women with both strongly nurturant and strongly dependent tendencies, nurturant toward those younger and frailer than themselves, dependent toward those older, stronger, or more authoritative than themselves.[28] Family and social life represent the major arenas in the lives of these homemakers, and, like the pattern of fifty years ago, the turning point in their lives is marriage rather than parenthood, following a very short period of time between school and marriage. They are fully socialized—indeed one might say overly socialized—for the assumption of marital and maternal roles. One suspects that these are the women occasionally overheard addressing their husbands as "Papa" and "Dad."

Pioneers, in contrast, have had looser ties with family and kin, have been oriented to the world of ideas and able to sustain less intense interpersonal relationships, have been free of the need to be dependent on others or nurturant of others. Their lower predisposition to nurturing is perhaps the reason they are less apt to enjoy being with young children. Being less predisposed to dependence, they are prepared to establish more egalitarian relationships with men, people older than themselves, or those in a position of greater

[28] It would be interesting to know if this generation's suburban homemakers experience a lack of social rootedness because they lack the extensive familial ties women of this type had for emotional sustenance in the more stable communities of previous generations. Contemporary young women have been reared with a high need for the continuation of close familial ties, but the increased geographic mobility of their husbands in this generation cuts them off from the people they have emotional need for. If their need for interperonal ties stems from such dependent motivations, it is little wonder that volunteer activities, political participation, or PTA meetings fail to fulfill them.

authority than their own. Since their own needs to nurture are less strong, their own personal expectations are for fewer children, with a greater willingness to sever kin ties and participate in the job world despite the responsibilities of home management and child rearing. Consequently the more crucial event in their lives is childbearing rather than marriage. This suggestion is supported by the profile of what the married pioneers were doing in 1964: 70 per cent of them were working, 25 per cent were going to school. Among married homemakers, in contrast, only a third were working and 2 per cent going to school of some sort.

Further support for the general interpretation offered can be seen in the contrast between the pioneers and the homemakers when they were asked to rate themselves in comparison with "other women of your age" on a number of personality characteristics. Pioneers are strikingly more apt than the homemakers to characterize themselves as "dominant" and "occupationally competitive," and homemakers take the lead in characterizing themselves as "dependent" and "socially competitive." But on only one of these self-descriptions is there a strong contrast between the single and married pioneer: the single pioneer is twice as likely as the married pioneer to say she is "occupationally competitive." One of the effects of marriage for pioneer women may be the blunting of their career strivings.

There are two other ways in which the general interpretation of the differential effect of marriage on pioneers and homemakers can be shown. One item in the questionnaire permits a classification of the women in terms of their general ideological position on sex roles, from a feminist position of more equality and similarity in the roles of men and women, to a traditional position stressing the differences between the roles of the sexes.[29] About one-fifth of the total sample took the feminist position, slightly less than a third took the traditional position, and not quite half took a more moderate position combining features of both points of view. This ideological item strongly differentiates the pioneers (half of whom subscribe to the feminist position) from the homemakers (40 per cent of whom subscribe to the traditional ideology). But when single women were compared with married women in each of these two career types, an interesting difference emerged: single homemakers are far more strongly traditional than married homemakers, whereas married pioneers are more inclined to take a "mixed" position than single pioneers. Once again, this suggests that marriage and family roles are less fully satisfying to the homemakers than they expected them to be, and that pioneers have found their career pursuits and living with a real husband rather than an idealized one a more difficult combination than they expected it to be. It suggests, further, that situational factors play an important role in the ideological values women hold concerning the social role of their own sex.[30]

[29] This item read: "Women vary a great deal among themselves on what they consider the most desirable pattern of life for women. Indicate the extent to which your own views approximate the "A" or "B" viewpoint:

"A. A *feminist* viewpoint, stressing greater equality and similarity in the roles of men and women than now exist, with greater participation of women in leadership positions in politics, the professions and business.

"B. A *traditional* viewpoint, stressing the differences between the roles of men and women, in which women's lives center on home and family and their job participation is in such fields as teaching, social work, nursing and secretarial service."

[30] It must be stressed that these are suggested rather than final interpretations of the research data, which may be modified or nullified by more detailed analysis. Undoubtedly some part of the pattern shown

Sex Differences in Views Regarding Women's Roles

One last strategy can be employed to illuminate the probable effects of marriage upon the life patterns and expectations of the pioneers and homemakers. It will be recalled that, in the Michigan State study, college men were more traditional and conservative than women. The NORC college graduate study gathered the responses of men as well as women to a number of items concerning women's roles in American society and the combination of work and marriage.

These data also show that men are more conservative concerning women's role than women themselves are. Since marriage probably involves more adjustment of the woman to the man's views than vice versa, here then is evidence supporting the general interpretation. On an item reading "Even if a woman has the ability and interest, she should not choose a career field that will be difficult to combine with child rearing," half of the women but two-thirds of the men agree. Again, although half the women thought it appropriate for a woman to take a part-time job if a child was a preschooler, only one-third of the men approved. A quarter of the men, but only 14 per cent of the women, thought a full-time job should not be taken until the children were "all grown up."

In another section of the questionnaire, the college graduates were asked to check how much need they thought there was in American society for certain social and political changes concerning women, recommendations stemming

---

in the text to differentiate single from married pioneers is not the "effect" of marriage, but a reflection of the fact that the most ambitious of the pioneers simply do not marry at as early an age as the less ambitious within their career type; and of course some portion of these single pioneers may not marry at all.

from the report of the President's Commission on the Status of Women, though they were not labeled as such in the questionnaire. On each count, men were between two and three times more likely than women to state that there was "no need" at all for the recommended changes: 23 per cent of the men, but only 8 per cent of the women, thought there was "no need" to make available "professionally supervised child care facilities for children of working mothers at all economic levels"; 36 per cent of the men compared to 18 per cent of the women thought there was "no need" to urge "qualified girls to train for occupations which are now held mainly by men"; 32 per cent of the men to 14 per cent of the women believed there was "no need" to encourage women to "seek elective and appointive posts at local, state and national levels of government." Here is indirect evidence not only for the direction of the effect marriage may have upon women's views, but for the likely reception women may experience as these young men move into policy positions in the occupational world as employers, educators, and colleagues of women.

Women themselves are keenly aware that quite different views are held by men than by women on matters that have a significant impact upon the lives of women. The women college graduates were given a brief account of a hypothetical family conflict and asked how they themselves would resolve it and how they thought "most wives" and "most husbands" would resolve it. In the story, a woman was graduated from college with honors in biology, married, and held a teaching job while her husband completed law school. Now he has a degree and a good job. Both wish to have children, but she would like to take an advanced degree in biology and eventually pursue a career in biological research. The women were asked what decision the couple should make: start a family now and have the wife get her training later; start a family now, and have the wife give up her research career plans; postpone starting a family and have the wife take a degree in biology; or carry out both wishes simultaneously.

Only *one-fourth* of the women thought the couple should start the family now, with the wife either giving up or postponing her training and career plans; but *half* of them believed these two decisions would be favored by "most wives" and *three-fourths* that they would be favored by "most husbands." When it is remembered that these are responses from all types of women, among whom the pioneers discussed earlier constitute a mere 7 per cent, it is clear that, regardless of whether women themselves wish to secure advanced degrees and pursue a research career, their sympathies are strongly on the side of the women who wish to do so.

There is reason to suspect that fewer husbands would favor the "family now" decision than women think would, since the contrast between the sexes is much sharper than on items for which there are actual responses from men college graduates. Some women no doubt are hiding behind the rationalization that they approve of certain career goals for women but do not pursue such goals themselves because men disapprove of women with higher career aspirations, and men are more important in their lives than careers are. Yet it is important to point out that such rationalizations are at work among women, and to indicate that men's attitudes must be changed as well as women's, if more women are to take professional careers seriously in American society. Women will not seek higher degrees in any great number in fields like the sciences and engineering, if by so doing they are punished socially and psychologically (or think they will be so punished, which can be a powerful psychological deterrent) instead of being rewarded as men are for their efforts and achievements.

Perceived Disapproval of Women in Selected Professions

The interpretation of the effect of marriage was based largely on inference: we argued that, because men in general take a more conservative stand concerning woman's role, marriage for women involves an adaptation to the prevailing masculine views. We can give some empirical substance to this inference, with data from another question in the schedule. Women in the college graduate sample were given a selected list of professions — architect, business executive, college professor, doctor, engineer, lawyer, and research scientist — and asked to indicate which of these professional jobs they disapproved of for women, as well as which jobs the following categories of people disapproved of for women: the respondent's husband (or closest male friend if unmarried), her mother, her father, most women of her age and education, and most men of her age and education. With these data, we can see the extent of the difference between the women in the sample and the men they are most intimately associated with, as well as their perception of sex differences in disapproval within their age-education stratum of society. The material is also of interest in providing educated women's impressions of how society views women's practice of certain professions.

First let us examine how the various people are ranked in their degree of tolerance of women in the professional fields on the list. At the top of the ranking in tolerance of women in this regard are the respondents themselves; 68 per cent claim they have no disapproval of women working at any of the listed professional fields. The next category is not the man in her life, however, but her mother (65 per cent no disapproval), her father (60 per cent no disapproval), most women of her age and education (59 per cent), and only then her husband or closest male friend (50 per cent) and, last, most men of her age and education, only a third of whom are seen to have no disapproval.

It is interesting that the women see their fathers as more tolerant and permissive of women who enter the masculine fields than their husbands, for it suggests a difference between the role of father vis-à-vis daughter and the role of husband vis-à-vis wife, a difference that is of importance in the cultivation of interests in things scientific and rational during the girl's formative years. In his role as father, a man is far freer to tolerate and to encourage his daughter in her pursuits into law, science, medicine, or even engineering, an encouragement he would not extend to his own wife, or to a woman as a younger courting man, for he would have to live with the consequences. If his daughter becomes a doctor or a scientist, he can feel pride as her father; whatever problems her career choice raises will not be his, as father, but hers and her husband's.[31] In all our focus on women, it

[31] It may even be congenial, psychologically, for some fathers with specially close relationships with their daughters, to encourage such intellectual career choices, for it reduces the likelihood and postpones the day when she will be not his but another man's. From this point of view, the father-daughter relationship may be cemented by the daughter's pursuit of a rigorous career goal. The mother-daughter relationship, unless the mother is herself a professional woman, may be negatively affected by the same pursuit in the daughter, partly because there is a growing gap of dissimilar interests and knowledge between mother and daughter, partly because the career-oriented daughter persists as a competitor for the father's attention and interest. This may be partly why college girls so often report that their mothers begin to draw limits on their aspirations once a college degree is assured. It is fine if the daughter does well, up to the college degree; beyond that, the mother would prefer that the daughter come back to a more traditional female role. It is interesting in this connection to note that,

must be remembered that, from the man's point of view, he may seek less in a wife than a wife wants in a husband for the simple reason that he can expect to find stimulation and intellectual comradeship in his work and with his work colleagues, an outlet many women do not have and therefore seek to fulfill in part through their husbands. It is easier to be the father of a bright and ambitious woman than it is to be her husband.

The specific professional occupations on the list were ranked in roughly the same order of perceived disapproval, whether the woman was reporting her own views, those of her parents, her husband, or men and women of her age and educational attainment. The rank order is from a high level of disapproval of women business executives and engineers, followed by women lawyers, architects, doctors, to a low level of disapproval of women research scientists and college professors. Thus, for example, two-thirds report disapproval of women business executives, one-third disapprove of women lawyers or architects, one-quarter of women doctors, down to less than 10 per cent disapproval of women scientists and professors. The fields of special concern to the MIT symposium are therefore found at quite different points on the continuum of perceived social disapproval: engineering is the most disapproved, science the least, and medicine in between.

---

historically, the early women lawyers frequently received their initial encouragement to enter law from their fathers. See, for example, the revealing portrait of mother-daughter versus father-daughter relationship in Alice M. McClanahan, *Her Father's Partner: the Story of a Lady Lawyer.* New York: Vantage Press, 1958; and the finding of close father-daughter relationships among famous women mathematicians, in Emma H. Plank and R. Plank, "Emotional Components in Arithmetic Learning as Seen through Autobiographies," *The Psychoanalytic Study of the Child,* Vol. IX, New York: International Universities Press, 1954.

There is one interesting exception to this pattern, involving a reversal of business executives and engineers: the respondents tell us their mothers and most women disapprove of women engineers more than they do of women business executives. But when the women college graduates report the feelings of their husbands, their fathers, and most men, they reverse the order of disapproval: more disapproval of women business executives than of women engineers. I suspect these perceptions are accurate, for business executives as a group differ from engineers in a way that is of exceeding importance to men's views of women in the world of business, government, and the professions. Business executives are by definition persons in authority over others, something most men are very reluctant to permit women to exercise over them, just as fewer women than men have a preference for assuming authority over others, particularly if these "others" are healthy adults. The women college graduates show an awareness of these social facts of life when they report more disapproval on the part of men — their husbands, fathers, and most men of their age and education — of women business executives than of women engineers.

One interesting confirmation of the sex differences in attitudes toward women in supervisory or authoritative positions is shown in Table 10. The respondents in this study are federal employees at the higher civil service grades. Three-quarters of the men say they prefer a man as their immediate supervisor; at roughly the same high civil service grade levels, two-thirds of the women say the sex of their immediate supervisor makes no difference to them. But neither sex shows any preference for women supervisors, and the experience of having had a woman supervisor has only a slight softening effect on the attitudes of these federal employees.

TABLE 10 Sex Preference for Immediate Supervisor among Federal Employees, by Sex and Experience with Women Supervisors (in per cent)

Sex Preference for Immediate Supervisor	Women[a] Had Woman Supervisor	Women[a] Never Had a Woman Supervisor	Men[b] Had Woman Supervisor	Men[b] Never Had a Woman Supervisor
A man	27	37	74	84
A woman	3	1	1	—
No difference	69	61	25	15

[a] Civil Service grades 11–15 for women.
[b] Civil Service grades 13–15 for men.
(Source: The President's Commission on the Status of Women, *Report of the Committee on Federal Employment,* October 1963, Table VI-2, p. 113.)

Perceived Reasons for Small Number of Women Doctors, Engineers, and Research Scientists

The women college graduates in the NORC study were asked why they thought few American women enter medicine, engineering, or the sciences. Their answers suggest that quite different obstacles are at work in restricting women's choice of engineering as a career goal from those militating against the choice of a career in medicine or science. With three professional fields and seven specified reasons for women's not choosing them as career goals, the data require a detailed analysis, but a few of the major highlights can be briefly described here, with the details shown in Table 11.

The ranking of these reasons is roughly the same for medicine and science. The two reasons the women college graduates cited most frequently involve the difficulty of managing demanding professional work with home and child responsibilities, and the desire on the part of women for occasional and part-time work rather than a full-time

TABLE 11 Perceived Reasons for Low Representation of Women in Medicine, Engineering, and Science (in per cent)

	Doctor	Engineer	Research Scientist
A job in this field is too demanding for a woman to combine with family responsibilities	80	38	54
Women today want to work only occasionally and on a part-time basis, which they can seldom do in this field	48	34	38
Most parents discourage their daughters from training for such a field	33	57	33
Men in this field resent women colleagues	38	56	23
To enter this field before marriage restricts a woman's chance to marry	25	14	20
Women are afraid they will be considered unfeminine if they enter this field	12	61	23
Such a job requires skills and characteristics women do not have	4	24	6
Other	8	7	9
N	(14,356)	(14,500)	(12,393)
No Answer	1,307	1,163	3,270
Total *N*, weighted sample	(15,663)	(15,663)	(15,663)

persistent commitment to a professional career. This is particularly the case with medicine, slightly less so for research in science. There is very little tendency to associate either medicine or science with inadequacy of skills on the part of women, or with an image of these professions as so dominantly masculine that a woman who entered them would be considered "unfeminine."

Engineering shows a rather different profile of perceived reasons. The major reason women see as accounting for the low representation of their sex in engineering is that women are afraid they would be considered unfeminine if they entered it, and perhaps for much the same reason, the second reason frequently endorsed is that parents discourage their daughters from training for such a field. In short, engineering is viewed as a thoroughly masculine field, which parents do not want their daughters to enter, and a field in which men engineers resent the presence of women engineer colleagues. Unlike medicine and science, women also tend to believe that engineering requires skills and characteristics women do not have.

The "obstacles" women perceive concerning a choice of engineering as a career goal are thus factors operating much earlier in the life span than those concerning a choice of medicine or science. Parents discourage in their daughters while they encourage in their sons the interests and hobbies that precede, by many years, a choice of engineering as a career goal. A long childhood of learning "appropriate" sex role behavior militates against American girls' acquiring the interests and skills that might start them on a path leading to careers in engineering. In contrast, the barriers to a choice of medicine and science operate at a somewhat later point in the life span. These are fields rejected by young women because they believe they would conflict with family obligations, not that they are in conflict with feminine skills and interests.

Fragile as these data are, they provide a point of departure for a discussion of several important factors affecting women's participation in and contribution to the demanding professions. For one thing, they tell us something about the stereotypes women hold about these fields. Consider, for example, the fact that the major reason cited for women's reluctance to enter medicine is the difficulty of combining such a demanding job with family responsibilities. This may flow from an image of the profession that has outlasted its applicability. The medical profession has changed, but the public image of the doctor remains rooted in the past: he is a dedicated man, modeled on the general practitioner of horse-and-buggy days, on call night and day, seven days a week. This is the image perpetuated by some sectors of medicine itself, and, perhaps more to the point, by the mass media. There is no room in this image for the contemporary partnerships, group practices, increased specialization, staff appointments, restricted house calls, and so forth, which are increasingly characteristic of the medical profession. The training required to become a doctor is unquestionably hard for a woman unless she postpones marriage and child rearing until she has her M.D., but there are now many new opportunities for specialization, group practice, and hospital and clinical appointments in which the combination of home and job responsibilities is no more difficult than for most other professional undertakings. A pediatric partnership could tide a woman over her own restricted periods due to childbirth. A hospital staff anesthetist or pathologist may experience more flexibility of routine and shorter hours of work than a laboratory technician.

The same discrepancy between image and the changed nature of the profession may be at work for the engineer. The image of the engineer held by many women and their parents is of a rugged outdoor type, highly masculine, smoking an unfiltered cigarette in a plaid wool shirt amid noise and bustle and dirt. The image bristles with blue-collar associations. This is a decided barrier to the choice of the field by women, since there are always available to them the minimum aspirations of a clearly white collar job in sales or secretarial work. With such an image, engineering does indeed appear to be an "unfeminine" field and one in which very masculine men would resent the presence of women colleagues. Once again, the image may crowd out the more likely situation of a conservatively dressed designer working at a desk or drafting board in an air-conditioned, pastel-painted office.

Stereotypes are persistent things, but if we are seriously interested in attracting more women into medicine and engineering, it is surely worth while to correct these images and portray the contemporary doctor and the contemporary engineer in work contexts typical of today rather than yesterday. It may also be the case that too exclusive a focus has been placed on the *intrinsic* rewards of a career in these fields. Intrinsic rewards in terms of personal stimulation and satisfaction are of primary importance, but it would also be useful to gather testimony from the husbands of women now in these fields who have found marriage to such women a stimulating, exciting experience. Young women need exposure to women scientists and doctors as models of what they might themselves aspire toward, but they also need exposure to men married to such women, as models of the kind of husbands they might have the courage to seek for themselves. And it may also be the case that men's attitudes would be far more amenable to change in response to the testimony of other *men* than to the urgings of women or government spokesmen for women to extend a welcoming hand to women professional peers or professionally active wives.

The image of the scientist is much more diffuse in the profile of responses shown in Table 10. These college educated women perceive little disapproval of women in science, and when they are asked to explain why there are few women scientists, no one or two reasons are heartily endorsed. This does not mean that there are no stereotypes of the scientist abroad in the land, but that college educated women may not share them. They have had recent exposure to science, science teachers, and men science majors in college, and, as we shall see later, they have nothing but the highest admiration for women who make notable achievements in scientific and scholarly pursuits.

One study conducted in the 1950's[32] is based on essays thousands of high school students wrote in response to uncompleted sentences concerning science and scientists. The results suggest that there is indeed a positive, official image of the scientist: he is a brilliant, dedicated human being whose patient researches lead to medical cures, provide for technical progress, and bolster our national defense. There are negative sides to this image as well, for part of the composite profile of the scientist includes the following: a man who wears a bulky white coat and works in a laboratory, is elderly or middle aged, and wears glasses. He is small and sometimes stout, or tall and thin. He may be bald, may wear a beard, may be unshaven and unkempt. In other words there are many contradictory characteristics in the image of the scientist: an abnormal relationship to money such that he vacillates between being in danger of yielding to the temptation of money and fame and of starving because of his integrity; bald or bearded; short and fat or tall and thin. The common theme holding these things together is the image of someone who deviates from the normal and

[32] Margaret Mead and Rhoda Metraux, "Image of the Scientist among High-School Students," *Science*, *126*, No. 3270, August 20, 1957, 384–390. Cf. also: Purdue Opinion Panel, *High School Students Look at Science*, Report of Poll No. 50, Lafayette, Ind., November 1957; and Walter Hirsch, "The Image of the Scientist in Science Fiction: A Content Analysis," *American Journal of Sociology*, *63*, March 1958, 506–512.

average; not a Mr. Average Man but Mr. Extraordinary, far from the normal, friendly human being who lives like other people and gets along with other people.

The woman college graduate does not appear to share this image, but she *was* part of the heterogeneous environment of the American high school at a critical period of her life. Adolescent girls are more dependent on and responsive to others in their social environment than are adolescent boys, with the result that the girl may be more readily deflected from pursuing science and mathematics courses herself. College may subsequently modify and correct her image of the scientist, but by then it is too late for such a career choice for herself, and she is left with admiration for the women and men who do pursue such careers.

A significantly large proportion of the women college graduates endorsed the view that women do not choose medicine, engineering, and science because they cannot get part-time or intermittent work in these fields. This is only one of several points in the study at which women show their reliance on part-time work as a solution to the dilemma of combining career and child-rearing responsibilities. Where the field permits it and the woman really needs it, part-time employment may indeed be a good solution for tiding a woman over the very early years of child rearing. But there is an unfortunate tendency in the past few years to overstress part-time work as "the" solution to the contemporary woman's need for both personal fulfillment and societal contribution. Almost half the women in the college graduate study tell us they think it all right for a woman to take a part-time job when a child is under five years of age, but only 18 per cent approve full-time employment when a child is a preschooler. Even the small minority of pioneers who are training for careers in the more demanding professions show this marked discrepancy in approval of maternal employment: one-quarter of the pioneers approve full-time employment when a woman has a preschooler, but fully 60 per cent approve part-time employment at this early stage of child rearing. If our general proposition is correct, that the experience of marriage and family roles leads to a reduction in the career focus of the pioneers, then as more of these young women actually have young children of their own, we may predict a very much lower endorsement of even part-time employment a few years from now.

Earlier tables have already shown that, except for teaching positions in colleges and universities, women in the professional and technical occupations who are employed less than 35 hours a week are a very small proportion of the total number of women employed in these fields. Indeed, a sharper look at the nature of part-time work in the total labor force underlines further how few such jobs are available that meet the needs and desires of women with child-rearing responsibilities. With full-time employment defined to mean at least 35 hours a week for at least 50 weeks a year including paid vacation and paid sick leave, the U.S. Census data show a very marked sex difference in the proportion of the labor force that is working full time: 65 per cent of the men and only 36 per cent of the women with work experience during 1962 fit this definition of full-time employment. But this does not mean the majority of women are working on time schedules easily combined with home management and child rearing. Part-time work can be of a variety of types: working full time for part of the year, working part time all year, or working part time for part of the year. What many women want when they seek part-time work is a schedule of working for a part of the day and not at all during the summer, so that they can be home with their children when they are not in school. The census category that best approximates this pattern — part-time employment for between 27 and 49 weeks a year — is filled by only 6 per cent of all the women who were employed during 1962.[33] The college graduate women not only approve of, but hope themselves to find, a part-time work pattern that is still all but nonexistent in the present labor market.

There is a more fundamental question to be raised that is far more critical than the question of the availability of part-time jobs in the present labor market. What is the effect of withdrawal from her field for any significant number of years upon the creativity we may expect from a woman in the scientific and technical professions? That she will need some retraining and "rust removal" has been much stressed in recent years, and these are the functions fulfilled by programs and centers for continuing education for women. I think there is a danger that such centers institutionalize and lend further social pressure to the acceptance of the woman's withdrawal for a number of years, a pattern that should not be widely or uncritically accepted until we have better answers to the question concerning the effect this withdrawal has upon the contributions we may expect from her. If we judge from the dozens of researches Harvey Lehman has conducted on the relationship between age and achievement,[34] the answer to this basic question must be a qualified "not very much."

Lehman investigated the relationship between age and creative achievement in such diverse fields as mathematics,

[33] A *Report on Manpower Requirements, Resources, Utilization and Training, op. cit.*, Table B-16, p. 222.

[34] Harvey C. Lehman, *Age and Achievement*. Princeton, N.J.: Princeton University Press, 1953.

opera composition, chemistry, philosophy, creative writing, and astronomy, to name only some of the many fields he has inquired into. His data include measures on the sheer quantity of published work produced by hundreds of men in these fields, as well as measures of the quality of their work as judged by experts in their fields. Both the quantity and the quality of these published works were then related to the age of the individual scholars when they completed such work. Lehman's over-all conclusions are that the quantity of output is sustained quite well throughout the life span of these men, but the quality of output is strongly related to age: the peak of creative work varies among the fields he studied from the late twenties and early thirties for the sciences, to the late thirties for such fields as music and philosophy.[35] Though his task of trying to do the same analysis for women that he did for men was complicated by the fact that so few women have contributed greatly to the sciences (and the fact that a large proportion of the women listed in biographical dictionaries failed to reveal their birth dates), what analysis he could attempt showed that women's most creative years in science do not differ greatly from the creative years of men.[36] The most creative work women and men have done in science was completed during the very years contemporary women are urged to remain at home rearing their families.

The sheer empirical relationship between age and creativity has been rather well established by Lehman, but the interpretive question of what this relationship means pleads

[35] A more precise formulation of his findings, illustrated for chemistry, is as follows: "In proportion to the number of chemists that were alive at each successive age level, very superior contributions to the field of chemistry were made at the greatest average rate when the chemists were not more than 26–30" (Lehman, *ibid.*, p. 324).

[36] *Ibid.*, pp. 97–99.

for further research. Lehman himself offers little interpretation, though he comments that, since the best neuromuscular coordination and the best creative thinking occur most frequently at very nearly the same chronological age level, the suggestion is strong that the relationship taps some fundamental characteristic of the human organism. If the relationship meant that the most original work was done in the years immediately following advanced training, it could be argued that, if the training took place later, the creative contributions could accordingly be made at a later age. But since his studies include the work of men who lived in the 18th and early 19th centuries, when there was no necessary connection between university training and scientific contribution, and in fields that required no extensive formal training, this seems to be an inadequate explanation.[37]

Consequently, we must seriously raise the question whether women with the greatest potential for significant contributions to their fields will have lost the primary chance to achieve such creativity if they withdraw from their professional work for any prolonged time during their youthful

[37] Another interpretation would be that, after a certain number of years of intensive work in some specialized field of inquiry, the scholar loses the intellectual freshness of outlook that he had at an earlier age. To the extent that this pattern accounts for even part of the age-achievement correlation, interesting possibilities suggest themselves as devices for prolonging the creative peaks into the later years of life. One such device is a self-conscious shift to a new problem area or related science, which could have the effect of generating a new period of productivity and creativity with that freshness of perspective that may be important to scientific breakthroughs or artistic creations. Such problem or field shifts might then produce not one but several creative "peaks" in the career histories of scientists and scholars. Many middle-aged academic scholars and scientists who experience vague restlessness might find that a shift of specialty would produce a more gratifying intellectual renascence than most geographic shifts from one university to another.

years. This is not to suggest that no woman can make outstandingly creative contributions at a later stage of life, for we all know exceptions to this, but merely to stress that the probability of doing so is reduced. I think this is a point well worth bearing in mind in a period when women are enticed to believe that withdrawal from the labor force in their twenties, followed by part-time employment in their mid-thirties and eventful full-time employment in their forties is their modern panacea to the conflict in women's roles.

There is one last point I should like to make in connection with the arguments for and against part-time employment as a solution to the woman's problem. If we take an historical perspective on the changes that have taken place in the relationship between the sexes, I think we can detect a natural sequence of change from a traditional to an egalitarian relationship which follows the human life span. It is difficult to imagine an egalitarian relationship between husband and wife after twenty years of marriage unless there was an egalitarian flavor to their marriage during the first twenty years of their life together. In the same way it would have been impossible to change societal values concerning maternal employment without first having resolved the question of whether married women without children should work. Changes in the status of women and of the relations between the sexes tend to occur when they suit the needs of the society, which often means when they suit the needs of men. The traditional view of woman's role is always shelved for the duration of a war, during which women are praised for leaving their homes and holding down a "man's job" while men are in the military services. At the end of both world wars, fewer women returned home to traditional lives than had left their homes at the beginning of hostilities. A taste of independence and active engagement in the work of the world can have a heady quality to it. In the years since World War II, early marriage has been facilitated by married women's employment. And young women's employment has been of enormous help to their husbands' completion of advanced training. Men have secured professional and advanced degrees with the help not only of university and government stipends but of their wives' paychecks.[38]

There is no longer any debate about whether married women should or should not work. Today's dialogue concerns whether employment and motherhood mix or not. That conflict is involved on this issue can be seen by the varied responses obtained if you suggest, as I have,[39] that men should not become fathers unless they are willing to make sufficient room in their lives for their children. Today we tend merely to bemoan the absent father and observe that many young mothers have to do both the fathering and the mothering of their young children because their husbands are so absorbed in their work. Despite the fact that there is general agreement about the importance of the father in the emotional development of the child, one hears and reads few assertions that men should make more room in their lives for fatherhood so that women would have room in their lives for more than motherhood, and their children would have adequate and meaningful contact with their fathers during the years when such contact means the most to the children's development.

My main point here is simply this: the five, ten, or fifteen years during which the woman is at home rearing her children are years during which the marital relationship is being stabi-

[38] Cf. James A. Davis, *Stipends and Spouses: The Finances of American Arts and Science Graduate Students.* Chicago: University of Chicago Press, 1962.

[39] Alice S. Rossi, "Equality between the Sexes: An Immodest Proposal," *Daedalus,* Spring 1964, 607–652.

lized. When she seeks a return to professional life, neither she nor her husband will be the same two people they were before the arrival of children. The children's expectations of their mother and the husband's expectations of his wife have jelled during those years. When the woman seeks a return to professional life, it then requires far more reorientation on the part of all members of the family, including the woman, than would be involved if she remained an independent and active professional while her combined wife-mother role was in the making. In light of these factors, and the findings of Lehman, older women who return to the labor force are an important reservoir for assistants and technicians and the less demanding professions, but only rarely for creative and original contributors to the more demanding professional fields.

Personal and Social Characteristics Differentiating Professional Fields

Work plays so central a role in industrial societies that it is scarcely surprising that the study of occupations has a vast literature in psychology, counseling, sociology, and economics. This literature has proliferated enormously during the past ten years, as our national interests have sparked and initiated a wide range of researches aimed at developing reliable indices of creative scientific talent, as well as extensive programs to reduce talent loss due to inadequate academic motivation or the financial means to secure advanced training.

Much of the research literature is detailed and highly technical in nature. It is therefore necessary to be quite selective in dipping into it for our present purposes: first, to give a very broad overview of certain salient respects in which science, medicine, and engineering differ from other major professional fields in the abilities required for adequate and outstanding performance, and the values and personality characteristics that seem to be associated with such career choices as young people sort themselves out among the many possible fields of work they can commit themselves to; and second, to give a somewhat more detailed profile of the personal and social characteristics that are particularly characteristic of the scientist. Throughout, my concern will be for locating those characteristics that differentiate between the sexes and thus help to account for the low proportion of women who choose scientific and technical occupations as their career goals.

Occupational Values and Career Choice

A general sketch of the occupational values that characterize the various career fields that the college graduates in the NORC study were preparing for will be the device used to achieve our first purpose, that of indicating how scientists and engineers differ from lawyers, businessmen, social scientists, humanists, and the practitioners of the more service-oriented professions like social workers and health therapists. Though these data were gathered from college seniors and the measure of occupational values is a simple one, the results are consistent with the more detailed studies of interests and personality characteristics of individuals either aspiring to or actually working in these fields.

Table 12 shows the distribution of the college seniors' responses to the question used as an index of occupational values. Being helpful to others, working with people, considering originality and creativity of considerable personal importance in picking a job or career, all receive a high endorsement by the college graduates. In contrast, remaining in or getting away from their home town very seldom carried any weight in their choice of a career field. The nine most frequently endorsed values were examined by means of Yule's Q test to determine which ones represented essentially independent dimensions of values. Three such factors were isolated in this way, as follows:

TABLE 12 Occupational Values[a] of 1961 College Seniors (in per cent)

Opportunities to be helpful to others or useful to society	65
Opportunity to work with people rather than things	56
Opportunity to be original and creative	51
A chance to exercise leadership	41
Living and working in the world of ideas	39
Opportunities for moderate but steady progress rather than the chance of extreme success or failure	33
Making a lot of money	24
Freedom from supervision in my work	18
Avoiding a high pressure job which takes too much out of you	16
Getting away from the city or area in which I grew up	13
Remaining in the city or area in which I grew up	7
N	(3,387)
No Answer	10
Total N[b]	(3,397)

[a] Question read: "Which of these characteristics would be very important to you in picking a job or career?"
[b] Representative 10 per cent subsample.
(Source: James A. Davis, *Great Aspirations*. Chicago: Aldine Press, 1964, Table 1.4, p. 12.)

People: "Opportunity to work with people rather than things" is strongly related to "opportunities to be helpful to others or useful to society," moderately related to "chance to exercise leadership," and essentially independent of the remaining items.

Original and creative: "Opportunities to be original and creative" was strongly related to "living and working in the world of ideas" and moderately related to "freedom from supervision in my work" and a "chance to exercise leadership."

Money: "Making a lot of money" is positively related to "a chance to exercise leadership" and "freedom from supervision in my work," and negatively related to "opportunities to be helpful to others or useful to society."

There are many extremely interesting differences in the value profile of many specific professional and technical occupations; these details may be found in the work of James Davis.[40] A general summary suffices for our present purposes. People-oriented values are highly endorsed by those headed for education, medicine, law, and the social sciences; moderately by those headed for business and the humanities; only slightly by those headed for the sciences and engineering. Values stressing originality and creativity are highly endorsed by those headed for the humanities, engineering, physical sciences, and social sciences; moderately by those preparing for education and the biological sciences; least of all in the fields of business, medicine, law, and other professions. Making a lot of money is most highly valued by those headed for business and law; moderately by medicine, engineering, and physical sciences; very little by those headed for education, social sciences, humanities, and biological sciences.

From this, we can summarize the value profile of certain of these fields. Engineering and the physical sciences show similar profiles: a high stress on originality and money, and

[40] James A. Davis, *Great Aspirations, op. cit.* Cf. particularly pp. 12, 31–41, and 172–185.

a low stress on working with people. In contrast, education shows a high stress on working with people, moderate on originality, and low on making money. Business and law show still another profile: a moderate-to-high focus on people-oriented values, low on originality, and high on making money.

Women are very high in their endorsement of people-oriented values and the stress on originality, but low on money, a value profile highly related to career choices in the humanities, education, social sciences, and other health professions. Men, in contrast, are far more often characterized by a value profile stressing originality and money, but low on orientation toward people, a cluster characteristic of those who choose the natural sciences and engineering.

This brings us to a fundamental question concerning value differences between the sexes. Why do women, compared to men, show such a strong orientation to working with people, a relatively weak concern for money, and a focus on originality and creativity that is high during the years of their schooling, and so often attenuated in the years that follow? To focus more specifically on the natural sciences in discussing this question, let us consider some further characteristics of the scientist with this question in mind.[41]

[41] In doing so, two caveats must be noted: for one, there have been no detailed psychological studies of women scientists with which we can gauge the extent to which women scientists differ from men scientists. Studies of students' interests and values suggest that field differences are far stronger than sex differences, with the result that women engineering students are like men engineering students, with interests in mechanical things, mathematics, science, and outdoor sports. Women law students share the profile of male law students, with high interest in verbal activity, writing, talking, debating, etc. Cf. Elmer Mitchell, "Interest Profiles of University Students," *The Vocational Guidance Quarterly*, 5, No. 3, Spring 1957, 95–100. But in drawing a portrait of the characteristics of the scientist, we do not

Characteristics of the Scientist and Implications for Women's Career Choices

Four factors have been found to be particularly characteristic of the scientist of note:[42]

---

know how and in what respects women may depart from this portrait when and if enough women reach positions of comparable eminence to those of men scientists who have been studied intensively.

Secondly, studies of the scientists on which the portrait relies most heavily were conducted in the 1940's with men then prominent as scientists. Whether younger men entering the considerably changed world of science in the 1960's and 1970's will differ we do not know, though a comparison of physics students with the physics faculty at a major midwestern university shows such striking similarity between their personality and social traits as to suggest little generational change. Cf. G. Stern, M. Stein, and B. Bloom, *Methods in Personality Assessment*. Glencoe, Ill.: Free Press, 1956. Yet there may well be room in the future world of science for many more different patterns of personality and social type, simply because scientists are now found in more diverse organizational contexts: in small academic laboratories as well as laboratories vastly more complex in terms of staff size, scope, and pace of work than was true only a few decades ago. Often scientists move into administrative positions of considerable authority, in government as well as in industry. Yet the scientist in industry shows many of the same marks as the academic scientist, and there is often strain between the "pure" scientists in industry and the product-oriented development researcher with whom he works (and dubs a "mechanic"), as has been shown in several organizational analyses of the scientist in industry. Cf. Simon Marcson, *The Scientist in American Industry: Some Organizational Determinants in Manpower Utilization*. Princeton University, Industrial Relations Section, Research Report Series No. 99, 1960; William Kornhauser, *Scientists in Industry*. Berkeley: University of California Press, 1962; and Anselm L. Strauss and Lee Rainwater, *The Professional Scientist, A Study of American Chemists*. Chicago: Aldine Publishing Company, 1962.

[42] This brief profile is drawn primarily from the work of Anne Roe on eminent biologists and physicists, whom she has compared with eminent psychologists and anthropologists. Cf. Anne Roe, "A Psychological Study of Eminent Biologists," *Psychological Monographs*, 65, No. 331, 1951; "A Psychological Study of Physical Scientists," *Genetic Psychol-*

1. *High intellectual ability,* with particularly high scores on tests of spatial and mathematical ability.

2. *Intense channeling of energy in one direction:* strikingly high persistence in the pursuit of work tasks, to the point that most are happiest when working.

3. *Extreme independence,* showing itself in childhood as a preference for a few close friends rather than extensive or organized group membership, and preference for working on his own; in adulthood as a marked independence of relations with parents and a preference for being free of all supervision, roaming in work where his interests dictate.

4. *Apartness from others,* with extremely low interest in social activities, showing neither preference for an active social life nor guilt concerning his socially withdrawn tendencies.

Let us now go back over these characteristics and examine them with an eye to the likelihood, or actuality where known, that women will have these characteristics as frequently as men. Since all these characteristics have their roots in childhood relationships and experiences, this procedure comes close to the basic sources of sex differences in early experiences that predispose one to scientific interest and its cultivation later in adolescence and early adulthood.

High Intellectual Ability[43] *and Independence.* For a con-

---

ogy Monographs, 43, May 1951; "Psychological Study of Research Scientists," *Psychological Monographs,* 67, No. 2, 1953; "Crucial Life Experiences in the Development of Scientists," in E. P. Torrance (ed.), *Talent and Education.* Minneapolis: University of Minnesota Press, 1960; "Personal Problems and Science," in C. W. Taylor (ed.), *The Third University of Utah Research Conference on the Identification of Creative Scientific Talent.* Salt Lake City: University of Utah Press, 1959, pp. 202–212; and *The Making of a Scientist.* New York: Dodd, Mead, 1953.

[43] This brief description of sex differences in intellectual ability relies heavily on the work of Eleanor E. Maccoby, "Woman's Intellect," in

siderable number of years it was assumed that there were no sex differences in intelligence, for, in study after study that relied on the Stanford-Binet intelligence test, practically no differences were found between boys and girls. An important point had somehow been lost to sight among psychologists, i.e., that in standardizing this test, items that revealed consistent sex differences were discarded because the test constructors were trying to create a test on which the scores of both boys and girls could be evaluated against the same norms.[44] Secondly, the Stanford-Binet is a test of general intelligence with a high stress on verbal ability. During more recent years, as specific tests have been constructed to tap different dimensions of intellectual and creative ability, consistent sex differences have begun to emerge.

From the results of these more highly specified tests, the following picture emerges. Perhaps because the developmental timetable is faster for girls than boys during childhood, girls do seem to be slightly ahead of boys: they talk at slightly younger ages, put words together into sentences somewhat sooner, count accurately sooner than boys; in school, learning to read seems to be easier for girls than boys, and fewer girls have reading problems requiring remedial help. This edge enjoyed by the girls disappears rather quickly: after the fifth or sixth grade, studies show boys doing as well as girls in reading comprehension, though girls show somewhat greater verbal fluency.

Seymour M. Farber and Roger H. L. Wilson (eds.), *The Potential of Woman*. New York: McGraw-Hill, 1963; and the bibliographic review of sex differences prepared for the Social Science Research Council: Roberta Oetzel, *Selected Bibliography on Sex Differences*, Stanford University, 1962 (mimeograph).

[44] Quinn McNemar, *The Revision of the Stanford-Binet Scale: An Analysis of the Standardization Data*. Boston: Houghton Mifflin, 1942.

In mathematical skills, there are no sex differences during the early school years, but during high school, boys begin to excel girls, and, by the time they take the Scholastic Aptitude Tests as applicants for admission to college, the boys score an average of 50 points higher on the mathematical portion of the tests, and girls score only 8 to 10 points higher on the verbal portion of the test. Whether this reflects the fact that girls less often elect advanced mathematics courses than boys, or that girls lack certain abstract qualities of intellective ability that are required in these mathematical tests, is difficult to tell. Maccoby concludes that the evidence leans toward the second alternative, since throughout grade school boys excel in "spatial" tests — e.g. detecting a simple figure embedded in a more complex one, or telling how many surfaces there are on the side of a pile of cubes which the viewer cannot see, findings which suggest that "boys perceive more analytically, while the girls are more global, more influenced by all the elements of the field together." [45]

These results suggest that, on the average, girls develop cognitive abilities along somewhat different lines from boys, and that they enter early adolescence with a style of thinking less appropriate to scientific work than that of boys. Although the final interpretation of this sex difference awaits further research, what is known is that the key to the difference between boys and girls lies in the kind and degree of independence training the child receives in childhood. If

[45] Maccoby, *op. cit.*, p. 29. Dyer also presents evidence from College Entrance Examination Board test result analyses, suggesting that even among the science-oriented students, who presumably have all taken considerable mathematics and science in high school, the boys still show higher scores in the mathematics test than the girls. Cf. Henry S. Dyer and Richard G. King, *College Board Scores: Their Use and Interpretation*, No. 2, College Entrance Examination Board, 1955.

a girl is encouraged to assume initiative, to solve problems for herself, she tends to develop the same analytic abilities as the boy typically does.

Maccoby cites one last convincing set of data on this point: pointing out that some children's scores on standard intelligence tests become higher over the years of formative development whereas the scores of others remain constant or decline, she draws a general picture of the child at age six who is among those whose IQ will increase by the time they are ten: "competitive, self-assertive, independent and dominant in interaction with other children. The children who show declining IQs during the next four years are children who are passive, shy and dependent." [46] These two sets of characteristics also tend to differentiate girls from boys, women from men, and among women, the homemakers from the pioneers.

Some of these sex differences persist even among men and women who have chosen the same occupational field in adulthood. That women are more often found teaching science than doing science may in part reflect this. In fact, studies of college teachers have shown that what women mention as satisfying them most about their campus jobs are "good students" and "desirable colleagues," whereas men teachers stress "opportunity to do research" and "freedom and independence." [47] In stressing the interpersonal side of campus teaching, the women reflect not only less independence of thought but their psychological dependence on comfortable relations with other people, both peers and the young. In a recent article in *Science* by a chairman of

[46] Maccoby, *op. cit.*, p. 33.

[47] Ruth E. Eckert and John E. Stecklein, *Job Motivations and Satisfactions of College Teachers*, U.S. Department of Health, Education and Welfare, Office of Education, Cooperative Research Monograph No. 7, 1961.

a biophysics department, the author generalizes his observations of the differences between male and female graduate students in his field. One of the strategies he has found successful in combining the roles of laboratory scientist and department chairman is to keep a laboratory assistant, because the sheer fact of having such an assistant means he will feel internal pressure to remain in close daily touch with the progress of research in the laboratory. He urges, however, that such an assistant be a woman, explaining his reason in these terms:

> The purpose of this assistant is to require daily instruction about what to do. Thus you are inescapably forced to plan for the operation of another pair of hands. A *female is better because she will not operate quite so readily on her own, and this is exactly what you want*[48] [italics mine].

The inference is strong, therefore, that behind the fact that few women are represented in science is the difference in cognitive style of male and female, which is in turn the result of differences in the ways girls are brought up compared to boys. If we want more women to enter science, not only as teachers of science but as scientists, we must encourage the cultivation of the analytic and mathematical abilities science requires. To achieve this means encouraging independence and self-reliance instead of pleasing feminine submission in the young girl, stimulating and rewarding her efforts to satisfy her curiosity about the world to the same extent her brothers' efforts are, cultivating a probing intelligence that asks why and rejects the easy answers instead of urging her to please others and conform unthinkingly to

[48] E. C. Pollard, "How to Remain in the Laboratory though Head of a Department," *Science*, 145, September 4, 1964, 1018–1021.

social rules. A childhood model of the quiet "good" sweet girl will not produce many women scientists or scholars, doctors or engineers. It may produce the competent meticulous laboratory assistant "who will not operate so readily on her own" as Pollard describes her, but not the creative scientist as Anne Roe has described him, for whom nothing else matters once intellectual independence is really tasted.

These are rather sober conclusions, for the problem of increasing the proportion of women in the sciences appears far less easily solved if one must change the social climate surrounding the young child than it does if one could merely rely on such institutional levers as increasing stipends and child-care facilities, retraining older women, changing our tax laws, or making symbolic appointments to high offices in the federal government.[49] How much hope is there, one may ask, for efforts directed at changing the ways in which parents rear their sons and daughters, or the ways teachers deal with boys and girls? Can one reach parents and teachers and change their view that science is for boys and not for girls? That sensitivity and independence are the necessary ingredients of creativity in both boys and girls? That sensi-

[49] This decade is one in which many doors are opening to bright and ambitious professional women, often with the support and by the policies of top governmental agencies, universities, and major industrial employers. But it must be realized that many of the present opportunities for adult women can only aid in implementing their choice of science as a career, not in helping greatly increased numbers of girls and young women to make the choices in the first place. Unless this is realized, many quarters of policymaking a decade from now may conclude that women do not want to, or are not able to, become professionals and intellectuals in large enough numbers to warrant continued special opportunities for them. See the examples of exclusive stress on broad institutional levers affecting adult women's participation in the labor force in recent editorials on women in science and engineering, which appeared in *Science:* 145, No. 3628, July 10, 1964, and 145, No. 3639, September 25, 1964.

tivity in sons should be encouraged and no longer considered unmasculine, and independence should be encouraged in girls and no longer considered unfeminine?

One experimental study by E. Paul Torrance[50] offers some encouragement in this regard. One of his researches into creativity involved assigning tasks to small groups of fourth, fifth, and sixth graders, to figure out the principles underlying a set of science toys. Many girls were reluctant even to work with the science toys, protesting that they "were not supposed to know anything about things like that." As a result, the boys demonstrated and explained about twice as many ideas as the girls did in experiments involving these toys. The research did not stop here, however, for Torrance initiated a series of conferences with the teachers in the school, and the parents of the children, explaining the results and pointing out the way in which girls are cheated of an important opportunity to learn and understand science, something desirable in itself in the complex technological world they will be part of as adults. The experiment was repeated the next year, after these conferences, and the results were quite promising. This time, there was no reluctance on the part of the girls to become engaged in the tasks, nor were they different from the boys in the enjoyment they expressed in the task, nor in their scientific knowledge. The mean performance of boys and girls was almost identical. In only one respect did the differences between the sexes remain unchanged. Both boys and girls thought the contributions the boys made were better than the contributions

[50] Cf. E. Paul Torrance, "Changing Reactions of Preadolescent Girls to Tasks Requiring Creative Scientific Thinking during a Thirteen-Month Period," *New Educational Ideas,* Proceedings of the Third Minnesota Conference on Gifted Children, 1960; and E. P. Torrance, *Guiding Creative Talent.* Englewood Cliffs, N.J.: Prentice-Hall, 1962, pp. 111–113.

the girls made. Pleasure and knowledge were positively affected; apparently group evaluation of the latter is harder to change. In any event, an experiment of this sort, which combined research and social action, is extremely encouraging to those concerned with changing the social climate surrounding the young girl.

Work Persistence and Apartness from Others. Prominent among the conclusions Anne Roe has drawn from her studies of eminent scientists, as it was from Cox's much earlier study of geniuses,[51] is the following: one of the hallmarks of the eminent men is high but not necessarily the highest intelligence, combined with the greatest degree of persistence and intense channeling of the individual's energies in his work. High intelligence is a necessary but scarcely a sufficient condition for a career in research science, for a great degree of persistence must be coupled with that intelligence.

That women with advanced degrees have sufficient intelligence to equip them for significant contributions to the fields in which they have worked is scarcely open to question. Self-selection works so much more strongly among women that, at each higher level of education, women probably have a greater potential for significant achievement than men. Since many more men than women go on for the Ph.D., one thing this implies is that the woman with an M.A. probably represents better potential than the male with an M.A.; yet women at this level still do not advance as far, earn as much, or achieve as much as men at their educational level. Studies of women with the Ph.D., like that on some 400 Radcliffe Ph.D.'s,[52] show that women publish sub-

[51] C. S. Cox, *Genetic Studies of Genius.* Vol. II. *Early Mental Traits of Three Hundred Geniuses.* Stanford: Stanford University Press, 1926.

[52] Radcliffe Committee on Graduate Education for Women, *Graduate Education for Women.* Cambridge, Mass.: Harvard University Press, 1956.

stantially less than men of comparable jobs and rank. That this is not attributable just to the greater home responsibilities of the women is supported by the finding that married women had published as much as the single Radcliffe Ph.D.'s.

I believe that a major clue lies in the differences between the sexes in the two further characteristics of work persistence and apartness from others. Both these characteristics mark the eminent scientist, and both involve factors which women are not encouraged to have in our society. It is a much rarer social phenomenon to find women than to find men with either extreme persistence and intense channeling of energy in professional work, or tolerance of and preference for social isolation. The one is related to the other, for persistence in work can scarcely combine easily with a high need for interaction with others, or with a social world in which others make high demands for interaction.

Let us look, with a young girl's eye, at the two figures of most importance in her early life — her mother and her father. Mother is someone always available, easy to interrupt, who takes care of a thousand details of home and family life yet in no logical sequence of order. In recent years, mother has become even more "instantly available" in our homes of contemporary design: her traditional territory of the kitchen has been invaded by family-togetherness nooks, or the kitchen may be only a corner of the family room. Yet father may have a room reserved for himself, a study or den, used only at night, and often out of bounds to the children except by special invitation. "Be quiet, father is thinking" is far more apt to be the child's experience than "be quiet, mother is thinking." The girl is more apt to have demands put upon her for housework and child-care assistance than her brother, and her parents are more likely to feel concern about any tendency on her part to social withdrawal and solitary pursuits than they feel for their sons.[53] Her "social popularity" is an asset to be cultivated and is again something considered more important for the girl than the boy, for he will be the chooser, she the chosen.

In this context, then, there are meager grounds for a girl's cultivation of persistent work habits or a preference for apartness from others. A young girl with high intelligence and scientific interests must come from a very special family situation and must be a far more rare person than the young boy of high intelligence and scientific interests. If she reaches adolescence with the same intellectual inclination, it is often despite her early family experiences rather than because of them. This may be why such women, when questioned in college about the background of their science interests, frequently point to particularly important teachers they had, often as early as the third or fourth grade, who stimulated and challenged them to stretch their minds. Alice Dement, in a study of women science majors,[54] points to the signifi-

[53] It is interesting in this connection that Knapp and Goodrich's study of the origins of American scientists finds their early habitat was often a midwestern rural or semirural community. Cf. R. H. Knapp and H. B. Goodrich, *Origins of American Scientists*. Chicago: University of Chicago Press, 1952. Not only is there less intense social stimulation by the sheer fact of lower population density in these environments, but a seasonal rhythmic adaptation of a man and his family to their ecology means the parents are often intensely busy with field and produce, and the child is left alone for long uninterrupted hours. These may well be the social grounds on which persistence was cultivated, for both the child's adult models and the long stretches of hours to himself are fruitful grounds for the development of introspection and the pursuit of solitary activities. A bright child in this environment then grows up with respect for and experience of both work persistence and apartness from others.

[54] Alice L. Dement, "What Brings and Holds Women Science Majors," *College and University*, 39, No. 1, Fall 1963, 44–50; and "The

cance of unusual, curiosity-arousing early environmental experiences: thus, for example, a daughter of a builder of small boats grew up surrounded by things mechanical and marine. In most such circumstances, what might have resulted was a fine flair for sailing. In this instance, she was intensely curious about what makes a boat run, an interest shared and encouraged by her father. The result: she was graduated from MIT last year with a major in naval architecture and marine engineering, and has taken a position in the research department of a company that is building submarines for the government.

To suggest that girls should be encouraged to be less dependent on others and to feel less need than they do for close ties with other people is sure to be met with considerable resistance and skepticism in many quarters. It is a recommendation made in a time when the tenor of our society is rather strongly in the direction of "social adjustment," smooth relationships with others, responsiveness to the opinions of others. Whether described in terms of the dominance of other-directedness by David Riesman, or in the more recent language of a shift from traditional to emergent values, as Spindler, Getzels, and Bidwell have described it,[55] recent studies have shown an increasing acceptance among young people of the stress on sociability, the relativist quality of morality and values generally, an excessive readiness to take on the coloration of the social environment and the views

---

College Woman as a Science Major," *The Journal of Higher Education*, 33, No. 9, December 1962, 487–490.

[55] George D. Spindler, "Education in a Transforming American Culture," *Harvard Educational Review*, 23, Spring 1955, 145–153; Jacob W. Getzels, "Changing Values Challenge the Schools," *School Review*, 45, Spring 1957, 92–102; Charles E. Bidwell et al., "Undergraduate Careers: Alternatives and Determinants," *School Review*, 71, No. 3, 1963, 299–316.

of others.[56] Some tendency toward social chameleonism may be the price we pay for the burgeoning of bureaucracy in our society. But the intellectual minority of the society who carry the burden and pleasure of creativity in the sciences as in the arts must work hard to resist this trend. When one reads in science education journals that many young people with scientific interests tend to be one-sided in their interests at the expense of all-round interests and social adjustment,[57] one worries that the educator or the psychologist who tries to help these young people become better adjusted may, in so doing, rob them of what would otherwise feed into persistence in scientific work and the willingness to run counter to public and scientific opinion, which is precisely what the creative person must do if he or she is to stretch and expand the walls of our knowledge.

Anne Roe has suggested that the kind of person who has gone into social science may have had a biasing effect on the theories produced by social scientists, particularly concerning the desirable or mature personality. She points out that a need for intense personal relations is one of the characteristics of social scientists themselves, who then exaggerate the importance of these intense personal relations as a basis of

[56] A very good illustration of this shift was shown in the longitudinal study of college students at Michigan State University; one effect of four years of college education is a reduction of traditional beliefs and an increase in emergent values. Cf. Dorothy Robinson Ross, *op. cit.*

[57] Thus one reads comments like the following: "the science-oriented pupil, whose voluntary work in microscopy, chemistry, radio or geology occupies much of his free time may cut himself off socially from his age group and not receive the maximum educational advantages that the school can offer. Guidance must take into account social, emotional and intellectual growth of the potential scientist. It must consider him as a person as well as a potential technician." From Herbert S. Zim, "Opportunities for Pupils with Unusual Science Talent," *Bulletin of the National Association of Secondary School Principals*, 37, January 1953, 156–165.

good social adjustment for everybody. Yet the physical scientists and biologists whom she studied indicate that an extremely useful and deeply satisfying life with adequate personal adjustment is not only possible but probably quite common among these scientists, with little of the sort of personal relations that psychologists consider essential.[58] When we realize that the currently crucial fields of education and vocational counseling are steeped in social science thinking and psychological assumptions, this is indeed cause for reflection and concern.

Success as a Woman: A Concluding Note of Encouragement

I should like to conclude with one last result from the NORC study of women college graduates, for it may help to dispel the somewhat pessimistic note inevitable in any coming to grips with the basic sources of women's low representation in the sciences and professions.

There are a number of different paths that women can pursue toward "success" as a woman in American society. Women may be noted for their figure and dress, the décor of their homes, the prominence of their husbands, and the accomplishments of their children, as well as through achievements of their own by winning awards for artistic, scientific, or scholarly merit, or by successful election or appointment to important positions in voluntary or political organizations.

If we ask, which of these different kinds of success do college-educated women admire the most, and which would they like to have for themselves, an answer can be given, for

[58] Anne Roe, "Psychological Study of Research Scientists," *op. cit.*, pp. 50–51.

these qeustions were asked of the women college graduates in the NORC study. For themselves, the picture is clear: it is to live in the shadow of the accomplishments of their husbands and children. The kind of success most often desired for themselves is to be the "mother of several highly accomplished children" and the "wife whose husband becomes very prominent." On the other hand, very few women college graduates chose such body-focused success as "Miss or Mrs. America contest winner," "outstanding film, stage or TV star," or "one of ten best-dressed women in America." Nor do these women show much interest in becoming prominent for their volunteer or political participation, despite the pleas of their educators that these are spheres of activities important for women to work in and easy to combine with home duties. Fewer than 5 per cent showed any interest in success as a prominent leader of a voluntary organization or as a national figure holding an elective or appointive political office. When it is remembered that these are responses to a question asking not what they realistically expect, but what kind of success they would most like for themselves, it throws into sharp focus the tendency of women to define themselves in terms of their intimate affiliation with other people rather than in terms of their own unique abilities.

But what is of extreme interest are their responses to the kinds of successful women they most admire. The kinds of successful women that these college alumnae admire most of all are women who receive scientific or scholarly awards, followed closely by women who receive literary or artistic awards. Close to four out of five women college graduates admire women with these particular accomplishments. The majority of the college-educated women in the United States may have opted against the serious pursuit of a demanding professional life for themselves, but they represent a sympathetic, admiring audience for the small minority of women who enter the now masculine fields and win acclaim for their accomplishments.

ENHANCING THE ROLE OF WOMEN IN SCIENCE, ENGINEERING, AND THE SOCIAL SCIENCES

JAMES R. KILLIAN, JR.

The status of women in America presents a number of striking contrasts and paradoxes. During the earliest days of the nation, American women had great freedom compared to the women of other nations.[1] Lord Bryce noted this when he wrote that, in the United States, "it is easier for women to find a career, to obtain work of an intellectual as of a commercial kind, than in any part of Europe." Yet in 1960 the Report of the President's Commission on National Goals emphasized that "the fullest development of every individual is hindered by underestimating the potential of a majority — women." Similarly, the report of the Rockefeller Brothers Panel Study, "Prospect for America," underscored

[1] See Carl N. Degler, "Revolution without Ideology: The Changing Place of Women in America," *Daedalus*, Spring 1964.

the need to take active steps to utilize this potential. "Many firms," it said, "still hesitate to use women in executive capacities or to include in an executive training program even those women who expect to remain in employment."

Yet we should not forget, as Henry M. Wriston noted in the report of the President's Commission on National Goals, that: "No women signed the Declaration of Independence. No woman participated in making or adopting the Constitution. Such an act would have been literally incredible. . . . Their change in status [since then] is a true revolution."

Higher education became available to women in significant numbers earlier in the United States than in any other country, but in 1964 Carl N. Degler was calling attention to the fact that, "in proportion to men, women have lost ground in America while gaining it in Europe," and that in the 1950's women received "about 10 per cent of the doctoral degrees in this country as compared to almost 15 per cent in the 1920's.[2] Today there are five women whose scientific accomplishments have been of such distinction that they have been elected members of the National Academy of Sciences. Most of these have been elected recently. Yet there are only five women out of 707 members.

Today there is widespread agreement that the nation needs to open more doors to women, particularly in the professions; yet we continue to tolerate many barriers to their advancement.

Almost every study that has been made of the uses of our human resources in the United States stresses the importance of better opportunities for women and deplores the small number of women workers in professional and semiprofessional occupations. In its report entitled "Women Power," the National Manpower Council noted that today

[2] *Ibid.*

one-third of all the women in the United States are in the labor force in any given month; yet women represent today a smaller proportion of our professional and semi-professional occupations than they did a quarter of a century ago. "Women now constitute a smaller proportion of all professional and semi-professional workers than formerly, largely because of the rapid increase in the number of engineers, nearly all of whom are men. In 1930, 15 per cent of all women workers were found in professional and semi-professional occupations and women constituted almost half of all workers in these occupational groups. In 1956, only 10 per cent of the women workers were in professional and related jobs, and they represented only 35 per cent of all workers in professional occupations." In short, as the population of the professional and semi-professional fields has grown in the United States, the numbers of women in these fields have not grown in proportion.

In its recent report, "Characteristics of Professional Workers," The Bureau of the Census gave further evidence of the declining percentage of women in science, engineering, and the social sciences. As summarized by Dael Wolfle, "In 1950 women constituted 1.2 per cent of all employed engineers; in 1960, 0.9 per cent. In 1950 women made up almost 12 per cent of the group of natural scientists; in 1960, only 10 per cent. In the social sciences the proportion of women dropped from 32 per cent in 1950 to 25 per cent in 1960." [3]

The Bureau indicated that in 1960 there were 7,714 women engineers, 14,616 women natural scientists, and 13,773 women social scientists. "Their median annual earnings from professional work were approximately $5,600 in engineering, $5,000 in natural sciences and $4,600 in social

[3] *Science*, 145, September 25, 1964, 1389.

sciences. The corresponding medians for men were some $2,500 to $3,000 higher." [4]

These are the contradictions and paradoxes that a conference of this sort must face frankly: everyone wants to see our great resource of womanpower more effectively used in professional fields, and yet the progress we are making toward this goal seems to be uneven and slow.

In preparation for this conference, I have done some sampling among some of our major corporate employers of professional personnel in the fields of science and engineering, soliciting answers to the following questions:

1. Are there growing professional opportunities in industry for women professionally educated in science and engineering?
2. Is it realistic to encourage young women to prepare for these fields if they are highly motivated and qualified?
3. What has been the experience of your company with women graduates in science and engineering?
4. Do you have a program for employing women for scientific and engineering jobs?

The responses to these questions are illuminating and tend further to point up the contrasts and paradoxes.

The attitudes toward the employment of women are favorable indeed. All the companies responding indicated that their experience with women scientists and engineers had been quite satisfactory. Yet the numbers employed are still very small. To the first question, "Are there growing professional opportunities in industry for women professionally

[4] *Ibid.*

educated in science and engineering?" the answers were strongly in the affirmative. One company noted that more than half its female employees who held degrees in science and engineering were hired during the past five years. Another company noted that it had projected a rising trend over at least the next five years in its requirements for professional scientists and engineers. It noted, further, that "women can benefit not only by this absolute growth of requirements but also could easily fill an increasing percentage of available openings. The lack of a strong upward trend at present results not from current attitudes, but from a lack of applications from qualified women. We believe the trend of opportunities for women could be definitely up, but that the opportunities must be seized to become a reality."

Another company notes that "there is no particular increasing trend in the number of opportunities for women professionally trained in science and engineering. However, we, and I would expect other industries, will have increasing opportunities for women with mathematics majors to work in the computer programming field. [Our] laboratories, particularly, will be looking for a number of such people next year and the individual companies are on the lookout for a few women with mathematical training for such work. This field, of them all, is a fast growing one and appears to offer much opportunity for women. The fact that the [company] currently employs very few women trained in science and engineering is undoubtedly due to the relatively few women who have taken such training and are seeking career opportunities in their chosen field."

A letter from the personnel officer of one of our major national laboratories, who, incidentally, is a woman, makes the following observation: "Many women do not continue their education beyond the bachelor's level in science and engineering, and since most of our programs require advanced degrees, this necessarily limits the number of women available to us. This limitation is reflected in the extremely small number of inquiries the Laboratory receives from women for employment; in any given year we might expect fifty applications from women out of a total of perhaps fifteen hundred. Furthermore, the majority of these applications are from women trained in mathematics; very few women with whom we are in touch are trained in the physical sciences or in engineering.

"Only about five per cent of the staff are women, which I believe is caused by a shortage of qualified women rather than discrimination on our part. The women who are employed here contribute valuably to our programs; some of them have supervisory as well as technical responsibilities. We had several young women graduate students at the Laboratory this summer; hopefully they will join our staff when they have completed their graduate programs. A few women scientists and engineers who were previously employed as permanent staff and left to devote their major energies to family life now contribute to the work of the Laboratory on a part-time basis or as consultants despite other responsibilities. I cannot say that we 'seek women for scientific and engineering jobs'; we do seek qualified applicants of either sex and all applicants are considered on their individual merits and accorded equal consideration."

The officer of a major chemical company, with long experience in dealing with college graduates, stresses the importance of distinguishing among the different fields of science and engineering where the supply and demand vary greatly. "I shouldn't think," he says, "that one could lump mathematics and, say, . . . sanitary engineering and talk about opportunities for women in science and engineering in a way that would make much sense." He further suggests that "it might be fair and realistic . . . to pass on to the girls at some stage that they have a built-in disadvantage almost regardless of field. I think one of my associates, an executive in engineering research, put it rather well when he said that people are paid for both performance and potential. The girls tend to be suspect on the second count because, statistically, they so often just aren't there when the time comes. I doubt that this would be news to them." He further notes that, as for the women his company has employed, "their superiors have been satisfied and often more than satisfied with their performance and contributions, even when they have not stayed very long. The director of the [central research department] told me recently that the women scientists it has have definitely been a net gain. I have never heard of a case where the departure was welcomed."

In this particular company the number of professional women employed include 14 Ph.D.'s, 28 with a master's and 129 with a bachelor's degree. Of the 129, 68 are chemists and 6 are chemical engineers. This is out of a total college population of 17,500, including about 2,450 Ph.D.'s.

In response to my inquiry whether it is realistic to encourage young women to prepare for these fields if they are highly motivated and qualified, the corporate response again was positive and encouraging, though problems were stressed. The companies all emphasized the fact that they seek qualified personnel, regardless of sex, and that they find that women perform equally with men in the same job categories. One company emphasized that it has found the attitudes of management in its plants and laboratories toward the hiring of women to be improved over the past and extremely good at this time.

One company underscored the fact that "one of the problems involved in encouraging women to prepare for these fields, even if they are highly motivated and qualified, is the question whether they are really career-minded. To hire a woman engineer and then only have her stay with you three or four years, until she decides to get married and raise a family, is a very costly investment from the company's standpoint. Therefore, we attempt to determine before hiring such a woman whether or not she intends to stay with us and make a career of her work. I will say that those few who do come with us do a fine job.

"In spite of the short supply of scientifically trained women and our concern as to whether they will make it their life work, we actively recruit women for science and engineering jobs. In addition to recruiting at co-ed institutions, the [company] visits six women's colleges."

The reaction on the part of these corporate employers clearly reflects the growing opportunities for women in science and engineering, while at the same time pointing up the limitations that apply. As the National Science Foundation observed in its 1961 report, *Women in Scientific Careers*, "There would seem to be little hope for expecting that a greatly increased number of younger women will enter scientific careers unless positive measures are taken to stimulate interest and to provide suitable incentives for those women with an interest in science. Better counseling, the improvement of science education and of employment opportunity, and the arousing of a genuine interest in science — these and other steps can and should be taken so as to persuade both boys and girls to consider careers in science and technology."

Any examination of trends in the employment of women must be made against a background of recent social changes.

There has been a trend in recent decades to earlier marriages and more children. The peak years for the participation by women in the labor force is now in the late forties. Dr. Rossi has emphasized that in no society have so many women devoted themselves full time to children and the home as in America today. This is simply another one of the paradoxes in our current situation where there is an obvious desire on the part of an increasing number of women for professional careers along with a more demanding commitment to marriage and children.

Clearly, however, there is a great opportunity for productive employment of married women after their childbearing is over. I saw one statistic recently, indicating that the median age at which a mother has her last child has dropped six years in a very short time. This means, statistically, that she still has an average life expectancy left of 50 years.

From these statistical trends, employer comments, and general observations that I have presented, I draw the following conclusions:

1. The rapid growth of population in the professions, especially in science and engineering, will bring enlarged opportunities for women, although the increase in opportunities for women will not be in proportion to the increase in the total numbers of scientists and engineers.

2. Much remains to be done to increase the opportunities for women in these professional fields. Of first importance, more women must prepare themselves more adequately for the practice of science and engineering. At present, the declining proportion of women in science and engineering results mainly from the lack of qualified candidates. There must be more women with Ph.D.'s; there must be more women with unswerving career ambitions; there must be

more women who really want to achieve professional status in these fields on their own merits and staying power. And there must be something else. There must be a determined assault by women on the professions, an assault that is more than a romantic impulse, but is realistic and solidly based on competence and commitment. The desire for professional recognition must not be marked by dilettantism. Women must aspire to great distinction and high performance in these fields.

3. The role of women in the professions must be designed to be compatible with marriage and the rearing of families. Other speakers on this program will deal with this requirement, and I will only annotate their comments by saying that new arrangements must be invented so that women may have satisfying careers along with amply fulfilling their role as wives and mothers. This means, especially, that new and convenient ways must be devised so that women may have families and still continue their education. Especially must there be opportunities for married women to take up professional work again after having left it. Our educational system must provide opportunities for women to refresh, renew, and update themselves intellectually so that they can again perform professional work effectively. It is heartening to see a number of colleges and universities — Radcliffe, N.Y.U., Sarah Lawrence, Minnesota, Michigan — offering opportunities for women to continue their education after devoting themselves to their families.

Of greatest importance will be the attitude of women themselves. They must be sincere in their professional ambitions, willing to meet, without special privilege, the requirements for professional attainment, and ready to demand, given these attitudes, their rightful opportunity to be scientists and engineers if they wish. There still will be barriers, but these can best be surmounted by high performance and consistent purpose.

Our society must use all of its human resources to their full ability, and in the growing awareness of this requirement lie the growing opportunities for women in all the professions, and not the least in science, engineering, and the social sciences.

THE PRESENT SITUATION OF WOMEN SCIENTISTS AND ENGINEERS IN INDUSTRY AND GOVERNMENT

Richard H. Bolt

When a woman goes into science or engineering today, she enters a man's world — especially if she goes to work in the government or industry. At least, that is what the statistics say.

Among scientists and engineers, men outnumber women 10 or 20 or even 100 to 1, depending on the job. For engineers, the ratio of men to women is 50 to 1 in educational institutions and nearly 120 to 1 in all other types of employment combined, as is shown in Table 1.[1] During recent

[1] The ratios given in Tables 1–4 are based on data obtained from *American Science Manpower* 1962, a report of the National Register of Scientific and Technical Personnel, National Sience Foundation Report NSF 64-16; from the 1960 Census of Population, U.S. Department of Commerce, Bureau of the Census; and from personal com-

TABLE 1 Ratios of Men to Women in Science and Engineering

Type of Employer	Engineers	Scientists	Scientists and Engineers
Educational institutions	50	4.3	5
Industry, government, and all other employments	118	13	34
All employments	114	8	21

years these ratios have tended to get larger rather than smaller. For equivalent work, men earn higher salaries on the average; and men are much more likely to advance into the highest positions. Also, statistics obtained from opinion surveys reveal certain prejudices and inequitable attitudes against women in some professions, including science and engineering.

That is what the statistics say: it is indeed a man's world. But statistics tell only one side of a story, and prejudices in the past do not necessarily equate to attitudes in the future. As I see the present situation, it is one of dynamic change, of promise, of challenging and expanding opportunities for women scientists and engineers, in employment of many types, including positions in industry and government.

Accordingly, I shall discuss the situation in two different ways. First, I shall sketch briefly a statistical profile of "womanpower" as it is deployed in science and engineering today. The profile will give estimated numbers of women in different categories, relative distributions of these women among fields, employers, and kinds of work, and related

---

munications from the National Science Foundation. Also, unless otherwise noted, all figures given in this paper are consistent with those published in *Profiles of Manpower in Science and Technology*, NSF Report 53-23.

ratios of men to women. Some data on salaries will fill in another dimension.

Today's deployment, of course, reflects yesterday's forces; socioeconomic factors, cultural attitudes, and public policies at work in the past have combined to produce the employment market as we observe it now. So, in the second part of the paper I shall consider some of today's forces that are shaping the deployment of women scientists and engineers of tomorrow. These forces include actions the federal government recently has taken, especially in connection with studies made by the President's Commission on the Status of Women.[2] Other dynamic factors are the nation's expanding needs for highly qualified scientists and engineers, potential contributions that new science and technology, derived in part from advances in defense and space technology, can make to the solution of important social problems, a growing demand for teachers and an emerging pattern of mid-career education and training, and, of course, an increasing public interest stimulated by the holding of special symposia, such as this one.

In other words, the present situation in industry and government, as I see it, contains two distinct elements. One is the existing pattern of employment, which the statistics can describe. The other is a set of forces now inducing change, which can be made visible by empirical evidence concerning the working environment.

Women in the Professions

The professions divide rather sharply between those that engage mostly women and those that engage mostly men.

[2] *American Women. Report on the President's Commission on the Status of Women*, U.S. Government Printing Office, 1963.

Also, during the past decade the contrast between these two groups of professions has tended to increase somewhat.

Women constitute at least seven out of every ten persons employed as professional nurses, dieticians, nutritionists, librarians, and teachers in primary and secondary schools. Men constitute at least eight out of every ten persons employed as accountants, pharmacists, physicians, lawyers, and — we especially note — scientists and engineers. In fact, engineering, where only about 1 per cent of the positions are held by women, lies practically at the extreme in this scale.

Between 1950 and 1960, the number of professional, technical, and kindred workers in the country increased by about 40 per cent. The relative increase in women exceeded 40 per cent in several categories, including professional nurses, librarians, and teachers. In contrast, the relative increase was less than 20 per cent for pharmacists, lawyers, scientists, and engineers. In the natural sciences and engineering, the number of women increased by only about 10 per cent during the decade, though in the same period the total number of scientists and engineers was increasing by some 60 per cent.

The relatively large increase in the number of men scientists and engineers was caused in part by many technicians' upgrading themselves, through on-the-job training, and thus becoming professional workers, and also by the abnormally large number of men who were graduated from college around 1950, owing to interruption of their education during the war. Even taking these factors into account, however, we can see that science and engineering have not become any less a man's world, numerically speaking, than they were 10 or 20 years ago.

Professional Scientists and Engineers

This year in the U.S.A. about 1,500,000 persons are working as professional scientists and engineers. Within this number, about 70,000 are women.

The largest concentration of these women, about two out of every five, works in the life sciences, including biological sciences, agricultural and medical sciences, and psychology. About one out of every four of the women scientists and engineers works in the social sciences; one out of every five, in the physical sciences; and one out of every eight, in engineering (see Table 2).

In all these fields, men outnumber women by a considerable margin. The men-to-women ratios are about 4 to 1 in the social sciences, 4.5 to 1 in the life sciences, 17 to 1 in the physical sciences and mathematics, and 114 to 1 in engineering.

If we look more closely at the different categories of life scientists, we find more than one-half of these women working as agricultural and medical scientists. About the same

TABLE 2 Distribution of Women Scientists and Engineers by Field, 1960–1962

Field Category	Per cent Distribution of Women	Ratio of Men to Women
Physical scientists, mathematicians	21	17
Life scientists including psychologists	43	4.5
(biological scientists)	(8)	(7)
(agricultural, medical scientists)	(24)	(4)
(psychologists)	(11)	(3.6)
Social scientists	24	4
Engineers	12	114
All fields	100	21

number of women are working as social scientists. These agricultural, medical, and social scientists, taken together, constitute almost one-half of all women scientists and engineers. The remaining scientists, working in the more "basic" natural sciences, numbered about 25,000 women in 1960 and reached about 30,000 this year.

Next, let us ask how these women, working in the natural sciences, are distributed among different types of employer — educational institutions, industry, and government. We can get a reasonable estimate of the distribution by drawing upon data reported by the National Register of Scientific and Technical Personnel for 1962.[3]

Educational institutions employ about one-half of all women working in the natural sciences, but only about one-fourth of all men working in these fields. In a reverse pattern, industry and the federal government together employ about three-tenths of the women scientists and nearly six-tenths of the men scientists. These contrasts have been sharpened during recent years. During the five-year period preceding 1962, the proportion of women scientists working in educational institutions increased from 47 to 51 per cent, while the proportion working in federal, state, and local governments decreased from 20 per cent to 18 per cent (see Table 3).

Another way to characterize the population of women scientists is to show how it divides among different kinds of work. About 37 per cent of these women work in research, 30 per cent of them teach, 6 per cent work in management, 6 per cent in development, production, and testing, and the remaining 21 per cent engage in other work of many kinds. Some of these figures contrast sharply with corresponding figures for men scientists. Management, for example, oc-

[3] *American Science Manpower 1962, op. cit.*

TABLE 3 Relative Distributions of Men and Women Nattural Scientists by Type of Employer

Type of Employer	Per cent Distribution for Men	Women
Educational institutions	27	51
Industry and business	45	18
Federal government	12	10
State and local governments	5	8
Other	11	13
Total	100	100

cupies 24 per cent of the men as against 6 per cent of the women. In the other direction, teaching occupies about 15 per cent of the men as against 30 per cent of the women (see Table 4).

TABLE 4 Relative Distributions of Men and Women Nattural Scientists by Kind of Work

Kind of Work	Per cent Distribution for Men	Women
Research	30	37
Teaching	15	30
Development, production, and testing	15	6
Management	24	6
Other	16	21
Total	100	100

Engineering Occupations

Women engineers number an estimated 8,500 this year, which is about one-fourth the number of women working in the basic natural sciences, and about one-seventh the number of all women scientists including agricultural, medical, and social scientists.

Occupational characteristics of engineers are quite different from those of scientists. A particularly informative profile of womanpower in engineering is obtained by using occupational categories as defined for census purposes. In the U.S. population census of 1960, about 870,000 persons were classified as engineers, of which about 7,600 were women. The categories into which they are divided relate more to types of industries and occupations then to types of employers.

One such occupation, for example, is labeled "College presidents, professors, and instructors." In 1960, this category contained about 3 per cent of the women engineers — 221 of them, to be specific. Another occupation, "Professional and related services," includes some engineers who work in colleges and universities, doing research and development. In all, about 400 or 500 women engineers are employed by educational institutions (see Table 5).

Another 20 per cent of the women engineers are classified under public administration and working in the federal

TABLE 5 Distribution of Women Engineers by Occupation, According to U.S. Census, 1960

Category of Occupation	Per cent Distribution of Women Engineers	Ratio of Men to Women
Manufacturing industries	41	140
Federal government	20	33
Transportation, communication, and other public utilities	14	70
Professional and related services	10	90
Construction industry	4	310
College presidents, professors, and instructors	3	45
Other	8	175
All occupations	100	114

government. Not all these persons qualify as "professional" engineers as we are using the term. Most of the women engineers work in industry: 41 per cent of them in manufacturing industries, 14 per cent in transportation, communication, and other public utilities, and 4 per cent in the construction industry. Other occupations listed include business and repair services, agriculture, forestry, and mining.

Within the total population of engineers, men outnumber women by 114 to 1. The ratio is more than 300 to 1 in the construction industry, 140 to 1 in manufacturing industries, 45 to 1 for college presidents, professors, and instructors, and 33 to 1 in the federal government.

Salaries

Salaries of women in science show two general features. First, the women who enter scientific professions earn more, on the average, than do their female classmates who enter other professions. Second, in any given field of science women earn less, on the average, than do men working in the same field.

According to a survey made by the Women's Bureau in cooperation with the National Vocational Guidance Association,[4] women who were graduated from college in June 1957 earned a median starting salary of $3,739 a year. Of the several categories reported, women chemists earned the highest salaries, with a median of $4,847, mathematicians and statisticians were next with $4,675, and then followed, in order, such categories as home economists, nurses, teachers, dieticians, secretaries, and typists. The highest and lowest median salaries were separated by more than $1,700.

[4] *First Jobs of College Women: Report on Women Graduates, Class of 1957*. Women's Bureau Bulletin No. 268, 1959.

A similar pattern was seen in a survey made in 1960 by the Bureau of Social Science Research for the National Science Foundation,[5] undertaken to study salaries of the 1958 graduating class after they had been out of college two years. Again the chemists were highest, at a median salary of $5,540, mathematicians were next at $5,520, and other categories followed in about the same rank order found in the earlier survey.

Average salaries for all workers in a field are, of course, higher than the salaries earned in the first two years. For example, women chemists in 1962 earned a median salary of about $7,000. For all fields of natural sciences combined, the median salaries in 1962 were $2,000 higher for men than for women, $10,000 as against $8,000.

The spread of salaries among different fields is illustrated by the following figures.[6] Median salaries in 1962 in physics were $11,000 for men and $8,000 for women; in psychology, they were $9,000 for men and $8,000 for women; and in chemistry and earth sciences, they were $10,000 for men and $7,000 for women.

In a "normal" labor market, we expect to see salary levels reflect the forces of supply and demand. We are not surprised, therefore, to find salaries in physics among the highest, because we know that physics research has been advancing rapidly and that competent physicists are sought for many kinds of work, in all sectors of the economy. Then why, we might ask, should women's salaries average $3,000 less than men's salaries in physics, but average only $1,000 less in psychology? This disparity cannot be explained simply in terms of relative supply, because women are con-

[5] *The 1958 College Graduate — Two Years Later.* Bureau of Social Science Research, 1961.

[6] *American Science Manpower 1962, op. cit.*

siderably more scarce in physics than in psychology. Women constitute about 3 per cent of all physicists and 22 per cent of all psychologists listed in the National Register in 1962.

Salary disparities such as these may be attributable to differences in academic preparation, or to the kinds of work that women are willing to accept, or perhaps to discrimination. In any case, we should have to go beyond the statistical curtain, as it were, and look at the employment practices in detail if we wished to gain a fuller understanding of the salary situation.

Employment in the Federal Government

As of October 1961, the federal government employed approximately 1,600 women in engineering, 1,500 women in biological sciences, 3,000 in physical sciences, 8,500 in mathematics and statistics, and 4,000 in social science, psychology, and welfare. These numbers cover all grades of government service and include subprofessional as well as professional workers.

Let us look at some historical trends. In 1938, the number of women employed in the federal government and working in science and engineering, all fields combined, amounted to about 2.7 per cent of all scientists and engineers. This figure had risen to 9.7 per cent by 1961. In engineering, the number of women increased from almost none in 1938 to 1.5 per cent of all federal employment in engineering in 1961. Over the same span of years, women in mathematics and statistics increased from 9 to 59 per cent (see Table 6). These figures come from lists compiled by the Civil Service Commission, and they contain essentially complete counts of all persons employed in federal service. In the several occupational fields listed, the categories used in the govern-

TABLE 6 Historical Trend in Federal Employment of Women in Science and Engineering, in All Grades Combined

Field of Occupation	Number of Women as Percentage of Total Employed in Year		
	1961	1954	1938
Engineering	1.5	0.4	nil
Mathematics, statistics	59.	15.	9.
Physical sciences	8.5	5.	2.7
Biological sciences	4.1	3.7	3.8
Social sciences	22.	13.	5.7
All fields combined	9.7	4.3	2.7

ment do not coincide exactly with those used in the National Register or in the census, and therefore the resulting statistics are not necessarily the same. Nevertheless, within the body of statistics available from the Civil Service Commission, we can find a great deal of self-consistent information to describe trends and distributions in federal employment of women.

We have noted that, in 1961, 59 per cent of the persons employed in the occupational categories called mathematics and statistics were women. Not all these women were professional mathematicians. Especially at lower grades in the Civil Service, many persons who work on mathematical and statistical projects possess less than full professional education, and they serve more as assistants than as independent professional workers. Specifically, in October 1961, federally employed women in mathematics and statistics numbered 1,035 professional and 9,716 subprofessional workers. For engineering, the figures are 248 professional and 1,314 subprofessional (see Table 7).

Although the Civil Service categories are not identical

TABLE 7 Federal Service in Science and Engineering: Division between Professional and Subprofessional Workers, as of October 31, 1960

Occupational Group	Subprofessional Total	Subprofessional Women	Professional Total	Professional Women
Engineering	47,452	1,314	57,974	248
Mathematics and statistics	9,716	7,503	4,671	1,035
Physical sciences	11,023	1,663	23,573	1,291
Biological sciences	12,337	626	22,502	861

with the categories used in the National Register of Scientific and Technical Personnel, we can compare data from these two sources and find that they give compatible information. For example, the Register shows that 13.6 per cent of persons working in mathematics and statistics were women; almost the same percentage is found in the federal government in Grades 12 and 13 combined. The relative concentration of women is about twice as great in the next two lower grades and only about half as great in the next two higher grades. Roughly speaking, we can say that federal employees in Grades 12 and 13, working in mathematics and statistics, represent about the same relative numbers of men and women as are found in the nation as a whole—at least as represented by the sample collected by the National Register. Similar correlations are seen for the other fields.

One way to interpret this information is the following. Starting at Civil Service grades of about GS 10 and running down to lower grades, we find an increasing number of women working in scientific occupations but who are not characterized as professional scientists and mathematicians as defined in the National Register. At the higher grades, on the other hand, the decreasing proportion of women suggests that it is relatively more difficult for women to rise to these higher positions in the government, regardless of their professional attainment. This inference is corroborated with information from other sources which indicates that in many cases women hold positions about two grade levels lower than men who have comparable educational and professional attainment.

The biological sciences stand out as an exception in certain respects. Over a wide range of Civil Service grades, the proportion of biological scientists who are women remains almost constant. Apparently, federally employed women in the biological sciences have attained a somewhat different status from that achieved by women in other fields of science. At all grades up to and including GS 15, and, in fact, running down to the lowest GS grades, women hold the order of 3 to 5 per cent of the positions in biological sciences. Does this mean that sex discrimination has been overcome in federal employment in the biological sciences? The statistics themselves cannot answer that question. GS 15 is the highest grade in the standard series of Civil Service positions. Above this level there are "super grades" GS 16 to 18, in which the salaries run from about $19,000 up to a ceiling of $24,000. At least until recently, no woman working in engineering and natural sciences have been promoted to these super grades. However, in the occupational category that covers social science, psychology, and welfare, about a dozen women hold positions in these super grades.

Professional employment in the government today starts usually at grade GS 7 for a person just out of college, and at GS 9 or GS 11 for a person who holds a graduate degree. Subprofessional employment ranges usually from G 4 to GS 11, thus overlapping professional levels somewhat. The salaries corresponding to the Civil Service grades are given in Table 8, as of October 1964.

TABLE 8 Federal Government Salary Scale, as of October 1964

GS 7	$6,050–$7,850
GS 9	7,220– 9,425
GS 11	8,650–11,305
GS 12	10,200–13,445
GS 13	12,075–15,855
GS 14	14,170–18,580
GS 15	16,460–21,590
GS 16	18,935–24,175
GS 17	21,445–24,445
GS 18	24,500–

The President's Commission on the Status of Women

During the past three years, the federal government has taken important new actions toward giving women equal opportunity to obtain employment and advancement on the basis of merit. Already some preliminary results of these actions are seen in the government record, and we may expect this federal leadership to produce results in other sectors of the nation also.

In December 1961, President Kennedy established the President's Commission on the Status of Women, and in this connection he sent to the Chairman of the Civil Service Commission a statement that contained these sentences:

> I believe that Federal employment practices should be a showcase of the feasibility and value of combining genuine equality of opportunity on the basis of merit with efficient service to the public. . . . I have, therefore, requested the Chairman of the Civil Service Commission to review pertinent personnel policies and practices affecting the employment of women and to work

> with the various departments and agencies to assure that selection for any career position is hereafter made solely on the basis of individual merit and fitness, without regard to sex.

Even before the Report of the Commission appeared in October 1963,[7] studies undertaken by the Commission had stimulated certain federal actions to ensure that appointments to government positions in the future would be made solely on the basis of merit and fitness. These actions produced immediate results: sex discrimination has been virtually eliminated from requests for new federal appointments. As for a long-term result, we may expect to see the government attract larger numbers of the more able women scientists and engineers and promote them to fill more positions at higher grades.

In order to assess the existing situation, the Commission, through its Committee on Federal Employment Policies and Practices, had a survey conducted to acquire facts and opinions.[8] Some particularly informative results came from survey responses given by a sample of about 11,000 women in grades 11 to 15 and about 3,600 men in grades 13 to 15.

How many of these persons had received promotions within the past two years? Forty-two per cent of the men and 24 per cent of the women.

How many thought that their prospects for promotion within the next year were poor or very poor? Twenty-four per cent of the men and 19 per cent of the women — the women were a little more optimistic.

[7] *American Women. Report on the President's Commission on the Status of Women.* U.S. Government Printing Office, 1963.

[8] *Report of the Committee on Federal Employment to the President's Commission on the Status of Women.* U.S. Government Printing Office, October 1963.

What were the reasons for thinking the prospects were poor? On this question there were large differences in views. About two-thirds of the men said there were "few opportunities" available — but only one in 50 women expressed that thought. Nearly one-half of the women who saw poor prospects for promotion felt that, if a man and a woman showed equal ability for a particular promotion, the man would be given the preference — that the woman must be clearly superior to the man. Apparently none of the men thought that women would be given preference.

About 15 per cent of the women attributed the poor prospects to another reason, that job requirements make it more difficult to place a woman, and presumably some of these requirements would have nothing to do with prejudice against women.

Although several years must elapse before major effects of the Commission's work become measurable, some preliminary results of these new moves are already seen. In obtaining persons to fill positions, agencies of the government make requests for certification from the Federal Service Entrance Examination. This is the main route through which the government employs persons of college level for professional and administrative careers. From November 13 to December 8, 1961, a period of one month just preceding establishment of the President's Commission, out of 454 positions requested, more than one-half of the requests specified either a male or a female to fill the position. Just three months later, between February 4 and March 3, 1962, of 694 requests, fewer than one in fifty specified the sex.

In four selected categories of civil service, the number of appointments made in 1962 increased above the 1961 figures by as much as 90 per cent for women and by less than 5 per cent for men.

The Commission also studied the situation of women in industry and other private employment. In addition to submitting general recommendations concerning equal opportunity, the Commission drafted, for consideration by the President, a proposed executive order that includes these words:

> . . . [Except for certain exclusions] . . . all Government contracting agencies shall include in every Government contract and the contractor shall include in his subcontracts the following provision: "It is the policy of the Federal Government that there shall be no discrimination against women in regard to hiring, training, and advancement in employment by reason of their sex. In the performance of this contract the contractor shall use his best efforts to comply with this policy." . . . Contracting agencies in awarding contracts shall give due attention to a prospective contractor's compliance with the policy respecting the employment of women and to the contractor's compliance with that policy in the performance of Government contracts.[9]

About how many women would this proposed policy affect? In research and development work alone, federal contracts with industry at present support about half a million scientists and engineers, of which 15,000 or 20,000 are women. This number of women would be eligible for equal opportunity in training and advancement, and no doubt the policy suggested would open up new opportunities and thereby would increase the numbers of women working in industrial research and development.

[9] *Report of the Committee on Private Employment to the President's Commission on the Status of Women.* U.S. Government Printing Office, October 1963.

The impact of the President's Commission on the Status of Women, including its several committees, marks a central element in the changing situation as I see it. Undoubtedly industry and other sectors of the nation will respond to this leadership, by striving for more equitable practices in their employment of women scientists and engineers.

Three Interviews

In order to get an up-to-date check on my thoughts regarding the situation of women scientists and engineers, I have talked with several of them about this subject during the past few weeks. Particularly relevant to my topic are some things I learned from these three women, one of whom works in industry, one in the government, and one in a combination environment, where she does research and development of an industrial nature in a government-sponsored center administered through a university.

All three of the women obtained bachelor's degrees, the earliest in 1951, the latest in 1959. Two of the degrees were in physics, one in mathematics. One of the women then got a master's degree in applied science, and the other two hope to get a master's or doctor's degree in the future. All three of them have taken further courses. All three hold regular, full-time positions and are highly regarded by their organizations. Their salaries run between $10,000 and $16,000, and correlate directly with number of years of work. One of the women is married, and the other two appear entirely eligible.

I asked one of the unmarried women, a computer programmer in industry, if she thought a woman's activities as a mother and homemaker would interfere with her opportunities in a career. "One good thing about programming," she said, "is that you can work part time. The girl who got me my first job is married and has three children. She does work at home, part time. I think it would be somewhat difficult to have a really full-time job with strict requirements, such as traveling; it would be very hard with young children. But once the children are seven years old, one can go back to work." Then I learned about an enterprising group that works in the Boston area, a team of some ten housewives who call themselves the Pregnant Programmers. I understand they are doubly successful.

The subject of technical management came up in my next interview, with a woman who was married three years ago and has completed about 12 years of continuous work. In an organization that employs more than 1,000 persons, she heads a subdepartment, in which 4 women and 5 men report to her. She also serves as deputy leader of a project, giving guidance to a project team of 4 women and 16 men. They work on design and implementation of a large-scale system.

I asked her, how did she, from her position of management, view the situation of women in her organization. "Women seem to be hired in (subprofessional) positions regardless of their experience. There appears to be some discrimination against women — it depends on whether a person has potential, and the feeling seems to be that no woman has potential." Then, how did she herself view the opportunities for women in her profession? She said, "The opportunities for women are excellent. Women can do an excellent job. . . . Women tend to be less creative [than men], but sometimes they are not given the opportunity to be creative." Then she suggested that women should be more aggressive than they usually tend to be. "Initiative will be recognized."

As to her own career, she saw no room for further advancement in this organization, but for a specific reason. "I have a combination of administrative and technical work, and anything higher would be mainly administrative. I would not want to do this, and I have reached a plateau in technical work." This particular response, I thought, could equally well have come from a man.

In the third interview, I talked with a women mathematician who works in a federal agency that supports scientific research through grants and contracts. In her work she evaluates proposals for research, keeps in close touch with research progress in her specialty, and coordinates her work with parallel efforts in other parts of the government. Partly because of the nature of her work, she was well informed about the topic we discussed, and she expressed some views that apparently are widely shared by women scientists in the government. In her words, "The opportunities for advancement for professional women, especially in the scientific area, are greater today than in any other period of time. This is probably due to two major factors. First, more women are entering into the scientific community, thus increasing the female percentage, and second, the prejudice which once existed against women, in what was once considered a strictly masculine area, has significantly decreased, and women are accepted and judged by the quality of their work and their competence in their jobs."

She described the organization of her agency, and pointed out that a woman now directs one of the eight major divisions, and at the next level down two branches are headed by women. Having these women in high positions ". . . is very advantageous to women who are starting in the field now. The scientific community is accustomed to dealing with competent women and this has done much to alleviate the prejudice."

Then she expressed a view that seems to be particularly

cogent. True, there are disadvantages to hiring women, "but there are also advantages, and these tend to balance out. One of the major objections is that they work a few years, get married, and stay home to raise their families. Thus, the employer feels that the training period he has invested in has been wasted. However, men change jobs too. From the employer's point of view it makes little difference whether an employee leaves to stay home or to work for another organization." Actually, this woman's opinion is that the turnover rate may be less for women than for men, at least in certain kinds of scientific work, and I think that a properly detailed study of her hypothesis would be worth making.

Summing up these three interviews, I see several similarities. All these women started with a good education (should I have mentioned that three of the four degrees came from Radcliffe, Smith, and M.I.T.?), and all have continued studying. All are working in fields that currently are advancing rapidly and are seeking good people. All three, I can report from independent evidence, are respected professionally, and their salaries — unlike the "median" salaries of women — are fully up to the salaries of men in comparable situations. And all three women attest to the dynamic change in which prejudice and discrimination are giving way to equal opportunity for professional accomplishment and satisfaction.

Defense Cutbacks and the Situation in Industry

A few months ago, a friend of mine who runs an engineering firm told me about the feelings he had experienced the week before when he called together a roomful of his professional staff to announce that all of them were being laid off. His experience is by no means an isolated one. In many parts of the country, especially where defense and aerospace work are concentrated, as in California and along Route 128, thousands of persons working in engineering have lost their jobs during the past year. Another friend has described difficulties he is having in trying to keep his remaining staff working effectively in the face of uncertainty regarding their own jobs. These are some of the personal, very real hardships that have been caused by cutbacks in defense spending and slowdowns in aerospace work.

Effects of these cutbacks have shown up also in a reduced demand for new engineering graduates during the year. One aviation company was looking for a dozen graduates in 1964, in contrast with 30 in 1963 and about 100 two or three years earlier. Some larger companies were hiring several hundred fewer professional people than they were a year ago.

In view of these facts, when many men are losing jobs or finding it hard to get their first jobs, how can a woman be optimistic about an engineering career in industry? My response is to cite some further evidence and let her be the judge.

First, some of the same companies that are hiring fewer new engineers this year are offering higher salaries. One university placement officer puts the average starting salary being offered engineering graduates in 1964 at $615 a month, up from $600 in 1963. Apparently these companies are trying to attract the most promising candidates, in order to enhance the quality of their staff and thus improve the company's competitive position in reasearch and development.

Second, some firms are actually hiring more engineering graduates in 1964 than they did in 1963. This pattern is seen in companies that are not dependent primarily upon defense contracts. Some of these companies work in traditional industries, such as chemicals and textiles, and others work in newer, science-based industries, such as computers. Undoubtedly these companies see in the present situation an opportunity to modernize their traditional business or to speed the growth of their new technological frontier.

Third, I observe some strong undercurrents running in the defense and aerospace industries and in the government agencies that support their work — undercurrents seeking new channels through which to apply government-developed capabilities to civilian markets. One such capability, for example, relates to the development of large-scale systems used in national defense, such as command and control systems and their associated facility for handling enormous amounts of complex information. This capability may find important applications to communication, transportation, medical services, and industrial processes. At the same time, high-level committees in the government are studying ways to help these industries convert some of their defense-generate capabilities into new channels of civilian need. It is too soon to judge how successfully such conversions can be made to work. But we can be sure that both the defense companies and the government are strongly motivated, for socioeconomic reasons, to conserve and utilize productively all engineering talent that is available.

As I read the evidence, then, the nation's engineering endeavor is going through a period of major readjustment; many companies are updating or redirecting their technological efforts; managers are trying to improve the quality of their staffs; highly advanced technologies, stimulated in large part by international tensions, now are available to serve human needs in yet undreamed-of ways; and the future, by which I mean within this decade, will bring unprecedented industrial opportunities for thoroughly trained, first-rate engineers — including women.

THE PRESENT SITUATION IN THE ACADEMIC WORLD OF WOMEN TRAINED IN ENGINEERING

JESSIE BERNARD

The topic assigned to me for this conference called for a discussion of the present situation in the academic world of women trained in science, medicine, and engineering. This is an eminently reasonable assignment, but it would take a whole volume to do it justice. And that, in fact, is what my recent book, *Academic Women*,[1] attempted to do. However, since there were so few women on the faculties in engineering schools, I did not include them in the book. Because the book is now available and because it devotes a great deal of space to women in science and in medicine, I am taking the liberty of not reproducing its contents here. I should like to refer to it when necessary but to concentrate now on engi-

[1] University Park: The Pennsylvania State University Press, 1964.

neering as an academic career for women. This is why the title of my paper reads simply, "The Present Situation of Women Trained in Engineering in the Academic World." But, taken literally, this title would not support a paper at all. A few sentences, perhaps a paragraph, is all that it takes to communicate the fact that as of now an academic career in engineering is not a very promising one for women. So perhaps I should change the title to read, "Bemused Comments on Some Quaint and Curious Nonengineering Practices among Deans of Schools of Engineering in Evaluating the Materials To Be Used in Designing Faculties for the Performance of the Several Functions Called for by an Engineering Faculty"? Or, if that strikes you as too long, how about "Demand and Discrimination"?

For I am called upon to analyze a situation in which there is apparently a burgeoning demand for teachers of engineering with a small supply of potential personnel to fill it, and at the same time a feeling on the part of young women that they are being discriminated against in the filling of these positions. As a caveat may I say that I speak as a sociologist who may know a little about sex roles but who makes no pretense of knowing about engineering laboratories or engineering education.

The Great Demand

There is an urgent thread running through much of the literature on engineering today that emphasizes the growing need for engineering talent. Your own Dr. Jerome B. Wiesner stressed the importance of using technical talent everywhere at the First International Conference of Women Engineers and Scientists last June, and Dr. Killian has told us of the growing demand for women in science and technology. The deficit in personnel is great, apparently, in all fields of engineering, but it is especially critical in teachers of engineering. One report, for example, has anticipated a deficit of 239,000 engineers by 1970, noting that ". . . the major divisions of the economy where especially rapid increases in requirements for engineers are anticipated include 'colleges and universities' . . . which may be expected to require about 90 percent more engineers in 1970 than in 1960."[2] And, as though to italicize the fact, the 1957 presidential address by Dean Everitt of the American Society of Engineering Education noted that "By all odds the most critical problem ahead of engineering colleges is that of finding a satisfactory answer — to where and how we are going to find, attract, train, keep and employ efficiently the many new engineering teachers needed."[3]

The need grows not only out of increasing numbers of students[4] but also out of the increasing demands that are made on faculties for research and consulting services at the expense of teaching. It is the students who pay for the services that faculty members perform for industry and government.

[2] "Review of Manpower Report of the President," *Journal of Engineering Education*, 54, October 1963, viii.

[3] Quoted by Robert W. Van Houten, "The Challenge Accepted," *ibid.*, 53, September 1962, 7.

[4]. The increase in students will be especially notable in areas for which, it would appear, women might be especially well suited, namely, research, development, and related activities. ". . . The accelerated growth of research for the next decade is so clear that one can hardly anticipate less than 50 percent of future engineering students desiring to be trained for engineering research, development and related creative activities." (L. E. Grinter, "The Research Objective in Engineering Education," *ibid.*, 53, October 1962, 77.)

Designing an Engineering Faculty: The Structural Properties of Women as Materials, or An Engineering Approach to the Uses of Women

Deans of engineering schools have the task of designing faculties for the several functions they are called upon to perform, especially teaching, research, and student counseling. They have, potentially at least, materials — men and women — of differing qualities. It seems to me there might be some engineering challenge in this problem.

Women as Material for the Teaching Function

Women constitute very good material for building a faculty; they tend to prefer teaching to research and writing. They would, it seems to me, be especially useful on engineering faculties where research and consulting take a big bite out of faculty resources. They tend to stay home and mind the store.[5] Academic men do so less and less. "I fear," says Robert W. Van Houten,[6] "that we in engineering education, as we have become more and more involved in research and as the requests for faculty members to do consulting have continued to increase, have forced teaching to assume a less important place in our educational structure. . . . Is it not possible that [research and consulting] are beginning to overshadow the vital importance of excellent,

[5] Charles Shilling and Jessie Bernard, *Informal Communication among Bioscientists*, Communiqué 16-63 of the Biological Sciences Communication Project, December 1963. This study of laboratory — not academic — scientists showed that women tended to be more sedentary and less likely to be away on scientific work than men.

[6] "The Challenge Accepted," *Journal of Engineering Education*, 53, September 1962, 7.

inspired, and dedicated teaching?" The answer is yes, but less so for women.

So far as ability to teach science and mathematics, as well as inclination, is concerned, the evidence — presented in *Academic Women* — is convincing. Women are displaying it today in colleges and universities all across the country. Women professors of mathematics, for example, as reported by a study summarized in *Academic Women,* were not as good as the best men teachers but neither were they as bad as the worst; they tended to hug closer to the average. No dean need hesitate to engage a woman to teach science or mathematics. She can do it. She is doing it. And at least as well as men.

It has been stated, however, that engineering teaching is more difficult than science teaching. In science teaching, it is alleged, there is usually only one solution; if students understand the principles, they can find answers. But "the engineer has to learn to work with situations in which there is no single answer and where deciding whether the design is sound and acceptable depends often upon statistical and judgment factors. . . ." [7] If this is so — and here my caveat about my ignorance of engineering education is relevant — it deserves some attention. For it appears, again from evidence presented in *Academic Women,* that women are most successful as teachers in areas where there is a standard, classic, authoritative body of traditional knowledge to be transmitted, a body that is increasing at a moderate rather than at a rapid rate. In medical schools, for example, anatomy is an area in which they are likely to be found. In colleges of liberal arts, they tend to be underrepresented in controversial areas such as political science and economics.

[7] Simon Ramo, "The New Pervasiveness of Engineering," *ibid.*, 53, October 1962, 69–70.

Whether there is any relevance of these findings to engineering teaching, I do not know. If it is true that the teaching of engineering — as distinguished from science — involves training in making judgments about the suitability of designs, it is possible that there may be sex differences. Conceivably women might be better in teaching judgment about some things and worse in teaching judgment about other things — assuming, of course, that judgment can be taught. I simply do not know. But I do know that there is a new area known as decision theory that can be taught and learned, and to the extent that it is applicable to engineering judgments, I feel confident that women can master it.

In any event, I am confident that there is a great deal of plain science and mathematics to be taught to engineering students. And here, I repeat, there is no basis for doubts about the suitability of women as materials for performing this function. Women can do it; they are doing it. In fact, they now carry a large share of the teaching at the elementary college and university level in the laboratory sciences and mathematics.

Women as Material for the Research Function: Strange Anomaly

A perplexing paradox struck me as I reviewed the position of women in technological schools. We are constantly being told that teaching is losing out to research in the academic status system. We are told that prestige adheres to the researcher and not to the teacher. And yet, strange as it may seem, in institutes of technology and engineering schools, women come in as researchers, not as teachers. At the California Institute School of Technology, for example, the 1964 catalog showed no women professors at any level, but 23 women in various levels of research, from associate to graduate fellow. At my own university, the lone woman professor in chemical engineering, Dr. Dorothy Quiggle, came originally as a research assistant. She became a professor, if not a teacher, when she took over the thesis work. (And now, alas, she is used primarily for administration, which reflects another anomaly, for allegedly administration also has more prestige than teaching.) Whatever all this means, it does not mean that women do not constitute good material for the research function of engineering faculties.

Women as Material for the Counseling Function

Quite aside from their intellectual contributions, academic women appear to be especially useful in dealing with students as people. They tend to be good in personal conferences with their students; many of them take a personal interest in their students. Such work with students is, according to one study of engineering faculties, an undervalued criterion for professional progress. This survey reported that "work with students outside the classroom" was felt by 70 per cent of the respondents to be given too little weight, and number of publications was felt by over half (56.5 per cent) to be given too much.[8] It is precisely this contribution to students that women are likely to be especially interested in and competent to make.

There would be an unexpected bonus for science and engineering if faculties took advantage of this special contribution of women, for concern for students, it appears, is an important factor in the recruitment of students into scientific careers. For example, in a study of 34,000 college graduates of June 1961, James A. Davis found a strong relationship between encouragement of students by faculty members

[8] "ECAC Comments on Young Faculty Affairs, Final Report," *ibid.*, 54, October 1963, 77.

and their career patterns. If faculty members encouraged students, the students tended to favor the subjects they taught. Incidentally, students report slightly less encouragement by science faculty members than by faculty members in letters." [9] If there were more women on science and engineering faculties, more encouragement might be forthcoming to students.

In brief, it would seem that, in designing a faculty for the most efficient performance of all the functions required of it, deans might well find women extraordinarily good material.

The Short Supply

Now that I have whetted the appetites of deans of engineering schools for women faculty members, I must immediately dash their hopes. Their visions of great teaching loads shifted to the shoulders of women must be tempered. The supply of women engineers is extremely small. The exact number and proportion of all engineers who are women are differently estimated by different observers. But however determined, both figures are minuscule.[10] Even though the

[9] James A. Davis, "College Experience and Choice of Science as a Career," Nontechnical abstract of paper given at the Philadelphia meeting of the American Association for the Advancement of Science, 1962.

[10] At a National Conference on Women in Engineering at the University of Southern California, October 15, 1963, a paper on the Report of President Kennedy's Science Advisory Committee on The Status of Women in Science and Technology, read by William Torpay, stated that there were fewer than 2,000 women engineers. He quoted Dean Alfred C. Ingersol to the effect that "only one quarter to one half of one percent of all the engineering talent in America today comes from the distaff side . . ." *Journal of Engineering Education,* 54, September 1963, p. 56. In "Why Don't American Women Go into

proportion of engineers who are women may have more than tripled between 1940 and 1960,[11] the fact remains that the number is still small.[12]

It might be argued that the number of women engineers is small because the number with aptitude for engineering is small. Still, on the basis of aptitude a somewhat larger proportion of engineers might be expected to be women. One study of 900 junior and senior high school students with high test scores for engineering aptitude reported that 7 per cent were girls.[13] At least that large a proportion of those with somewhat less aptitude must also be girls. A not unreasonable proportion of engineers who were women would seem to be about a tenth. A considerable number of girls with high aptitude for engineering do not enter that profession and are therefore not available in the pool from which engineering faculties may be drawn. Increasingly, also, it appears that engineering faculties require a doctorate. This new requirement restricts the available number of women

---

Engineering?" *American Engineer*, 34, August 1964, p. 31, S. Marczoch reported 7,531 women engineers in 1964. A discrepancy this large suggests differing criteria for selection.

[11] S. Marczoch (*ibid.*, p. 27) reported that 0.3 per cent of engineers were women in 1940, 1.0 per cent in 1960. This increase is difficult to understand, in view of the decline in number of bachelor's and first professional degrees conferred in engineering to women, reported by Beatrice A. Hicks, "Our Untapped Source of Engineering Talent." In Society of Women Engineers, New York, *Women in Engineering*, 1955 (Mimeograph), p. 38. Her figures were: 1947–48, 191; 1948–49, 158; 1949–50, 175; 1950–51, 87; 1951–52, 60; 1952–53, 37; 1953–54, 62.

[12] As noted above (S. Marczoch, *op. cit.*), only 7,531. The largest single number were industrial engineers, 2,266. The other areas were: electrical and electronic, 1,561; aeronautical, 778; unclassified, 726; civil, 700; mechanical, 557; chemical, 542; metallurgical, 279; sales, 101; mining, 21.

[13] *Ibid.*, p. 28.

even more; for only about four women at the present time achieve the Ph.D. in engineering every year.[14] Alas, the ravenous dean scouring the field for women to add to his faculty will find that they are very scarce.

Sigrid Marczoch suggests three reasons — cultural, functional, and social — for the small number of women in engineering: (1) the attitude that engineering is an all-male profession with no place for women, so that girls are counseled away from it,[15] (2) the unwillingness of employers to hire women only to lose them to marriage, and (3) certain social obstacles arising from sex differences in circumstances in which much engineering work must be done.[16]

The image of engineering as an all-male profession is a hangover from the time when engineering was understandably indeed a male profession. It was largely building and construction, often of military as well as civil installations. Today the trends in engineering favor the participation of women, since they are functionally in the direction of emphasis on design and research and substantively in the fields of aerospace and electronics, in none of which do women suffer drawbacks.

Whatever validity there may be in industry's reluctance to hire women only to lose them to marriage after investing in their training — and it may be challenged even here[17] —

[14] *Ibid.*

[15] It might well be the equivocal rather than the negative nature of the counseling girls received with respect to engineering that inhibits them. Dr. Dorothy Quiggle, for example, a professor in the College of Chemical Engineering at my university, was encouraged to apply at MIT by the President and Dean who talked to the girls at Latin School, but was discouraged by two professors when she did apply.

[16] Marczoch, *op. cit.*, p. 33.

[17] The reluctance of employers to hire women because they may lose them by marriage — I am told that some companies practically demand a vow of celibacy — seems to me particularly against engineer-

such reluctance is not equally valid for the academic world. For fortunately the academic world is learning how to accommodate itself to the career calendars of women. Old anti-nepotism rules which used to prevent wives from teaching are in process of attrition. Some schools are delighted to employ the wives as well as the husbands. Engineering schools might make their first step in recruiting women faculty members by engaging wives already available, especially, at first, in the fields of mathematics and science. In any event, it is surely contrary to engineering policy to refuse to hire women for fear of losing them to marriage; the truly engineering stance, it seems to me, would be one that sought to design a policy by which both engineering teaching and

---

ing in character. One would think that engineering industries would be among the first to design staff use that would take into account the material they had to work with, including women. Women are good material even though account must be taken of the probability, perhaps fifty-fifty, that they will need some sort of accommodation when they marry and have children. Extended maternity leave, perhaps, or part-time work. The problem should certainly not tax engineers accustomed to fitting design to material and making allowances for its special qualities. What I am trying to say is that perhaps a lot of the problems that we speak of as women's problems really belong to all of us. Why, for example, should women alone have to make all the adjustments called for by modern societies? If we need all these talented women workers, as apparently we do, why should we not ease the adjustments that they have to make? It seems to me quite wrong for employers to maintain an antiseptically know-nothing policy concerning the problems involved in the career calendars of women workers — or worse, an almost punitive one. It seems to me that a suitable position for employers to take would be that the problems of women are the problems of all of us. We are all in this together. We are in a mixed-motive, not a zero-sum game. We — employers and women — may both win or we may both lose. One would think that people who are inventive enough to design ways to get to the moon would be clever enough to design ways of helping women combine marriage, motherhood, and scientific contributions.

marriage could share the talented women. Other colleges have shown how it can be done.

Sigrid Marczoch's third reason for the scarcity of women engineers has only vestigial validity in this area. Whatever arguments might be raised against the suitability of some kinds of engineering careers for women, they would not hold for teaching. As Sigrid Marczoch has noted, it is understandable that there might be problems if a woman in an isolated part of the world had a crew of men to work with.[18] But the trends in engineering, as noted above, favor women; the newest fields do not call for work far from civilization where sex per se might be an important factor. And certainly teaching does not. In a highly civilized environment like that of an engineering school, this kind of difficulty can scarcely loom very large. Few, if any of the social obstacles invoked against the use of women engineers in some of the more traditional areas of engineering apply to academic careers.

That none of the factors which Sigrid Marczoch gives as reasons for the scarcity of women engineers is insuperable can be seen from the fact that about a third of the engineers in the USSR are women — I saw many of them myself in 1959 on dams and running textile mills; in Finland 11.2 per cent are women; in Norway 9.8 per cent; and in Sweden 9.4 per cent. And even in the Middle East, where the status of women seems to us low, 9.5 per cent of engineering students are women.

Discrimination?

Why is it that, in the face of such a great demand for faculty in schools of engineering and of a potential supply among women, the young women feel so strongly that they

[18] Marczoch, *op. cit.*, p. 30.

are victims of prejudice? In my assignment, the statement was made that "although people generally seem to assume that no prejudice toward women exists in colleges and universities, professionally trained women seeking employment, and even women entering graduate programs, often find the opposite to be true." I cannot speak here on prejudice, which refers to covert behavior, for I have done no research on it. But I would like to discuss discrimination, which is overt behavior.

The subject of discrimination on whatever basis — age or race as well as of sex — is extraordinarily complex, subtle, and difficult to be unequivocal about. Discrimination is extremely difficult to demonstrate, and evidence — for or against it — is not interpreted the same way by all observers. And here I would like to inject some puzzling facts.

While I was writing *Academic Women* I often discussed my findings with academic men. Their first reaction was that surely discrimination must be the major burden of the study. They assumed that the book must be a diatribe against discrimination, and most of them were apologetic or defensive. Actually, discrimination was only one theme, and not a major one, in the book — and very difficult to prove. The evidence suggested that women were represented on faculties in about the same proportion as they were in the qualified population from which faculties can be drawn. Awards seemed to be distributed among the sexes in roughly the same proportion as applicants. The Woodrow Wilson Fellowship program, in fact, reserves about a fourth of its awards for women despite the fact that the dropout rate for women doctoral candidates is greater than that for men. For academic women as a whole, discrimination was hard to document. Where it does exist, it is against the top-flight academic women. They are the ones who are victimized by it. And *Academic Women* documents this fact by a number of historic cases. Last June the top-ranking student in engineering at Pennsylvania State University was Miss Joanne L. Yamas, from whom I here quote:

> I started at Penn State majoring in chemistry. In my sophomore year I took a chemical engineering course "for fun," industrial stoichoimetry, to be specific, and liked it. I decided to go into chemical engineering since I like both mathematics and chemistry and this ties the two together. Another reason I chose chemical engineering was that at that time I wasn't sure whether or not I wanted to go to graduate school and from what I was told it is not as necessary to go to graduate school in the field of engineering as it is in the field of science.
>
> One of my sorority sisters at the time was also in chemical engineering and warned me about the switch. She told me how she used to be afraid of putting her first name on tests since teachers were so prejudiced against girls in the field. However, I really didn't find this to be true. The teachers at Penn State were more than fair to me. I think that once you show them you really want to work and aren't just interested in the fact that engineering is an "all-boy" curriculum, the teachers will go out of their way to help you. . . .
>
> When I applied to graduate schools I found very little prejudice. I was accepted by all the graduate schools I applied to including the University of California at Berkeley, the University of Wisconsin . . . , the University of Minnesota, Stanford, and several others, except for Princeton. I received a very nice letter from the head of chemical engineering at Princeton explaining that the only reason they could not accept me was the

> fact that I was a girl. From the other schools I received fellowship and assistantship awards.
>
> As far as obtaining jobs is concerned there is prejudice, for good reason, however. Companies do not want to hire a girl engineer, have her work for about three years and then get married and have children. They will, but the field truly is limited and with the same qualifications the man will of course be hired above the woman. . . .

What does it add up to? One girl feels there is prejudice, another does not. One graduate school rejects a brilliant candidate because she is a girl; half a dozen others offer her assistantships. No wonder there is little consensus on the subject.

Two very wise, experienced, and knowledgeable men read the manuscript of *Academic Women*, one my dean for 17 years — Ben Euwema — wrote a foreword and one, David Riesman — who knows more about academia than almost anyone else — wrote an introduction. Both men in effect rebuked me for my posture with respect to discrimination. They felt there was more discrimination than I had found; they chided me for lack of crusading zeal against it. David Riesman implied that perhaps I had been brainwashed so that I did not recognize discrimination when I saw it. He did not feel that the we-may-lose-her-by-marriage argument was legitimate; he saw the matter as a moral one.

Both these men have sat on committees selecting candidates of one kind or another, and they know intimately the processes involved. They have heard the criteria discussed, including the sex of the applicant. If they say there is discrimination against women in academia, it must surely be there. But it is very hard to prove. It is conceivable that men feel a strong prejudice against women but also that, feeling guilty about it, they lean over backward not to express it in their overt behavior.

In order to demonstrate discrimination, one has to know the criteria being used in selection. A bright young faculty man at a great university once said to me cockily, "Of course we discriminate against women." It so happened that there are very few women in his field. When I asked him whether he would recommend Dr. —— for a vacancy in his department, he said, of course he would; she was an established, prize-winning scientist who had proved herself. It turned out that he was thinking of young women, and what really determined his judgment was, indeed, as in industry, the chances of losing them to marriage. His argument was that a department head is playing a game against nature. One of nature's strategies is marriage for the young woman, so that the outcome of selecting her rather than a comparable young man has a lower pay-off. The question is, can this weighting of outcomes really be interpreted as discrimination? [19]

Marriage and Motherhood

Quite aside from the matter of discrimination, any discussion of careers of whatever kind for women has to take into account such facts of life as the probabilities of marriage and motherhood. For both engineers and academic

[19] Milton Eisenhower has said that it is estimated to cost Johns Hopkins University $200,000 to train every full-time professional woman biologist, a sum considerably greater than the amount to train men biologists. The figure was apparently arrived at by assessing the cost of training all the women biologists who left the profession against those who stayed in it. With such an accounting system, the admission of women to graduate schools would be very restricted. David Riesman, as noted above, rejects this whole conception.

women, the marriage rate appears to be extremely low. Sigrid Marczoch sketched the average woman engineer today as 36 years old and her chances of being married as fifty-fifty.[20] Academic women also have a very low marriage rate, especially those who teach in colleges. Thus those of you who look forward to academic careers in science or engineering are less likely to marry than the average young woman.

But do not be dismayed. I should like to point out that despite the enormous pressures that have played upon young women to marry, and fairly early, during the last generation, marriage is not necessarily the best design for living for everyone. I am certaintly not advocating that any of you take the veil — although that has something to be said for it in certain cases — but simply that you refuse to be frightened into marriage because of extraneous pressures. There is a great deal to be said for a celibate vocation; much of it is said in *Academic Women* by Vida Scudder, a pioneer professor at Wellesley. Unmarried women, in contrast to unmarried men, show up extremely well in surveys of mental health and in studies of general social adjustment. There are many women who live fulfilled, satisfying, and wholesomely creative lives outside of marriage. Marriage is just fine; I am certainly not against it. But marriage has become almost compulsive; young women feel that if they have not got a commitment by their senior year there is occasion for concern. It may be that this compulsion is relaxing somewhat. More young women are now going on to college and more even to graduate study. It may be easier to remain unmarried in the future than it has been in the immediate past.

But if even half of you marry, this probability has to be programmed into any discussion of career plans. If I were asked about this I would say, as Lois Barclay Murphy said

[20] Marczoch, *op. cit.*, p. 27.

to one of her students (quoted in *Academic Women*): choose the right husband. For it takes both husband and wife to make a career for either one. It is especially essential for career women to have the sympathetic support of their husbands.

Then decide whether you want to invest a big chunk of your life in your work or whether you want to reserve a fair chunk for other things. By and large, academic women are less likely than men to put all their emotional eggs in one basket; they tend to invest less of their lives in their work; they have other sources of satisfaction. If you want to commit less than a large chunk of life to your work, settle for what I have called fringe-benefit status — on the fringes of the profession but of great benefit to the institution that hires you. This means, in all likelihood, teaching beginning courses in laboratory sciences and mathematics. I do not know about colleges of engineering but, so far as other colleges and universities are concerned, I can assure you that you will have little difficulty. You will be welcomed with open arms. You may not have tenure; you will not exercise a great deal of academic power; but you will be respected and, best of all, you will feel you are in a rewarding situation. You will be able to help students and supply support for many who might otherwise not make the grade for other than intellectual reasons.

If you are willing to commit vast stretches of time to your work, spend hours in the laboratory or library, run very fast to keep up with new developments in your specialty, stick your neck out with new ideas, fight for them against vested interests, you may climb to the top of the academic ladder. A number of such women are described in *Academic Women*, and your guests at this conference are cases in point. It can be done. However, unless your husband — if you have one — is with you all the way, the going will be rough. In fact, you might do well not to encumber yourself with any other kind of husband than your work.

Although the rewards are great, if you have to pay too much for them, they may not seem commensurate with the effort. So it seems to me that the most important decision any young woman — or young man, for that matter — has to make deals with a scale of values. Know yourself, know what you want — not only that, but have an order of preference among the many things you want. If you want some things — all-absorbing work, for example — more than you want other things — marriage and motherhood, or vice versa — then you have to be willing to pay for them. In my course on the family I used to ask my students to scale their values, that is, not only to rank them, but also to determine as well as they could the intervals between the ranks. Such an exercise helps in planning one's life.

One final word. If or when your generation breaks the sex barrier in engineering schools and technological institutes, as it was broken in medical schools a long time ago, remember that it will be a new situation to the men you will have to relate to, both fellow faculty members and students. Help them. It will be harder for them than for you. You are better prepared than are the men for the change. If they haze you, take it in your stride, good-naturedly if you can, as Florence Sabin did at Johns Hopkins University. Above all, be yourself. If you are a very feminine person who loves jewelry, finery, and the like, do not smother it. But if you are the tailored or the casual type, do not think that you have to indulge in ruffles and bows in order to prove that you are a woman. You do not have to be like a man, a substitute or *ersatz* man. A department head quoted a letter he had received from a woman applying for a position on his faculty who said that she had been in her present job for ten years and so far as she could tell no one had acted as though she were a woman. He did not consider this fact an asset. Learn to endure with patience a certain condescension in men, as Americans in the nineteenth century had to learn to grin and bear it in foreigners. Have the courage to be just who you are. As such you have value. Have no fear. If you are groping — as you doubtless are — so are others of your age. As a matter of fact, so are all the rest of us, of any age.

I end with a statement from one successful academic woman in the Department of Electrical Engineering in a School of Engineering and Architecture. She says:

> I don't know if my colleagues accepted me happily, but accept me they did. Teaching is not a male profession, neither is engineering. I certainly never had any problems with the students. I think people should stop . . . [making] so much fuss about women in so-called professions; all that counts is performance and competence.

PART III

The Case For and Against the Employment of Women

Panel Discussion

THOMAS W. HARRINGTON, JR., *Moderator*

ACADEMIC EMPLOYMENT

WILMA A. KERBY-MILLER

SELF-EMPLOYMENT

MARION G. HOGAN

WOMEN ENGINEERS IN INDUSTRY

W. SCOTT HILL

RETRAINING FOR EMPLOYMENT

ELEANOR WEBSTER

GOVERNMENT INTEREST IN THE EMPLOYMENT OF WOMEN

ROBERT F. MELLO

ACADEMIC EMPLOYMENT

Wilma A. Kerby-Miller

I hope that many of you attending this symposium have given or will give serious thought to becoming teachers — either in a school or in a college. The present shortage of science teachers has been widely publicized, and, with the annual sharp increase in school and college enrollments in this decade, well-prepared teachers of mathematics and science are being eagerly sought at all levels of education from elementary schools to universities.

Elementary and secondary school teaching can be a highly satisfying experience for women who enjoy working with children and who believe that the reason that many children do not "understand" science and mathematics is that these subjects are all too often poorly taught in our schools. Moreover, a young woman who marries soon after receiving her bachelor's degree may find in school teaching her best opportunity for a career. There will be a high school in any community in which she lives, though there may not be an industrial laboratory or a college. Yet one annoying problem for a young woman who might be interested in high school teaching is meeting certification requirements. All states now require a few special courses in education for permanent certification of public-school teachers. There has been a good deal of criticism among students, as well as among educators in liberal arts fields, of courses in education, and, rather than take them, some students have given up the idea of teaching. It should be pointed out, however, that new programs in teacher training are beginning to replace the old, criticized ones. Courses in these programs are based on recent studies of the learning process by eminent psychologists and on new approaches to subject matter and curriculum planning in all fields. Students are finding the new courses far from easy, dull, and obvious. The history of education, for example, is just as exciting as any other history course when it is taught by a distinguished historian.

Excellent Master of Arts in Teaching programs are being offered in several of the leading universities in the country. In these programs up to one-half of a student's work can consist of graduate courses in her major field and the other half in training for teaching. Careful study and planning make practice teaching, which is at the heart of training, valuable and rewarding not only for the young teacher but also for her pupils. Among the universities offering Master of Arts in Teaching programs are Johns Hopkins, Chicago, Stanford, Rochester, Vanderbilt, Emory, Harvard, Yale, and Wesleyan. The program at Harvard, which I know best, draws many high-ranking students from an association of twenty-nine colleges in this part of the country and from other colleges in almost every state. It includes an excellent science program, for which extensive recruitment is carried on because of the need for science teachers. There is much flexibility and individuality in the planning of students' programs, with consideration for earlier work in a subject-matter field and for any previous preparation for teaching.

I have taken time to mention secondary-school teaching because I believe that it can be the answer to a career for many able women whose temperament and personal circumstances make doctoral degrees and positions in colleges or in research organizations difficult or impossible. College teaching is, however, probably of more immediate interest to most of you than is school teaching. Such a choice is only natural at this stage of your education, when the excitement of advanced work and research makes the idea of graduate study in your field and the teaching of older students more attractive than the thought of working at a more elementary level. If you would like to teach in a college, you should by all means plan to earn a Ph.D. degree in your field. You will need to look ahead to several years of hard work for the degree, but they can be interesting and valuable years both for learning and for living. Marriage may interfere with your progress, but marriage is becoming less and less an obstacle to graduate study and to a successful career in teaching. With determination and good luck in your choice of husband and place of residence, you should be able to find a very satisfactory college position.

College teaching holds many advantages for a woman scientist who wishes to continue with research in a professional way while she teaches. Her hours of classroom work are not overwhelming in number. Colleges and universities will usually provide her with space and facilities for research. If the college offers any graduate work at all, she will probably have first-year graduate students doing research under her direction. Because she is connected with an educational institution, she may more readily than otherwise be able to obtain government grants or other aid for her own special research. She enjoys an independence that a worker in a large research laboratory often does not have, and she can spend her summer vacations much as she pleases.

If a woman is a highly successful teacher and wins some recognition for her research, she has the possibility of advancing through the academic ranks to a professorship and to the security, prestige, and leadership that such a position brings. Although in the past the majority of women scientists who have achieved professorships in scientific as well as in other fields have done so in women's colleges, many universities with preponderantly male faculties now express a willingness to hire women for permanent positions if the women are highly qualified. According to a recent survey published by the National Education Association, about three-quarters of the colleges in the country indicate that they will employ women. They do not, however, indicate how many of their highest positions are now held by women, and one does not have to look very far to see that in many well-known universities women will have an uphill struggle to reach full professorial status. Indeed, the charge of discrimination against women in the highest academic ranks is not uncommon. In considering whether such discrimination actually exists to any formidable extent and whether it can be overcome, several factors need to be taken into consideration. One is the very small number of women who earn Ph.D.'s and, as a consequence, the very limited number of women available for advanced positions. In the past decade women have earned only about 10 per cent of all the doctoral degrees in all fields awarded in the country. One survey shows that, of a total of 1,995 students awarded Ph.D.'s or Sc.D.'s in physics in the four years from 1949 through 1953, only 35, or 1.7 per cent, were women. Last year only ten women earned Ph.D.'s in physics, as compared with 742 men. Numbers of Ph.D.'s are somewhat larger in biology, chemistry, biochemistry, and mathematics, but even in these fields the percentages of women are small — 4 per cent in all the physical sciences, 7.4 per cent in mathematics, and 12 per cent in the biological sciences. Another factor that may affect the availability of a well-trained woman for a teaching position is, of course, marriage and the consequent limitation on the area within which she can accept a position. Even when a university or college hires an unmarried woman, there is always the fear that she will not remain very long in the position — a fear that is often justified. It is also true that a married woman who has children cannot during some years compete with her male colleagues in producing the research which may be required for advancement to higher positions. All these situations are ones which not not only women but also society and academic employers must face and try to solve realistically.

Historically considered, the problem seems less discouraging. Women have, after all, taught in colleges in competition with men only in this century. If we can only increase the number of well-qualified women teachers, I am sure that there will be no lack of opportunities for their employment, even in institutions that have in the past been reluctant to hire women. Colleges are becoming more and more willing to hire both a husband and a wife if both have excellent qualifications, and, as more women earn higher degrees, this practice will no doubt become fairly common, though we may have to wait another century for it to be accepted by public institutions. Furthermore, the fact that women may not be able during their first years of teaching to produce as much research or as many publications as men do is gradually being accepted in academic circles and is not a deterrent to promotion when the understanding is that a woman will return to full scholarly activity after her children no longer need daily hours of care. Also, part-time jobs in colleges are beginning to give young married women opportunities to keep up and develop knowledge in their fields until they can work full time.

I sense in the present generation of students a seriousness about careers such as has not been prevalent since the early part of this century when it was not unusual for a girl to say that she preferred spinsterhood and a career in teaching to marriage. I am not suggesting spinsterhood, but I see in young women a growing realization that, if teaching is to be improved, they must help improve it. One can say, perhaps, that it is partly automation in the household that has brought on the new era, but it is also, I am sure, the great spread of education in this century. For a constantly growing number of women, intellectual pursuits are becoming an essential part of their lives. Teaching will provide for some of these women one of the best ways of learning, growing intellectually, and being of service to others.

SELF-EMPLOYMENT

Marion G. Hogan

My approach to the problem of employment in the sciences is a bit different, as well might be expected from my background and my activities. The program states that I am self-employed. What does this mean? It means that I cannot be fired. It also means and has meant that I have not been able to afford the time to study the statistics about the kind of work that I was interested in. Whether the ratio was 115 to 1 or a million to one made no difference to me. When I was graduated from M.I.T. in 1946, with a master's degree in meteorology, everyone said, "Don't try to go into industrial meteorology, you cannot make it pay." There were no such companies in existence in the country at that time. I have been in business for 19 years and there are now 100 industrial meteorological firms. In 1960 while visiting oil companies, being very inquisitive and observant, I scrutinized their methods of dispatching, and found them cumbersome and outmoded. I worked for a year and developed a system whereby deliveries to many thousands of customers today could be processed without machine equipment in five minutes tomorrow — a system based on just plain common sense. So I was not worried about odds, and neither should you be.

If you wish to be active in the field of science and engineering, and you will notice that I did not say if you want to be a girl scientist, prepare yourself academically first. There may be one-and-a-half million positions in engineering today, with only a relative handful of women in any of them, but as Dr. Killian has said, trained women are not available. You may talk of discrimination, but the lack of women scientists, I contend, is due not to discrimination, but to the lack of the encouragement of women to enter the field of science. There is no stronger weapon against discrimination of any kind, if discrimination does indeed exist, than numbers. I do not talk of sheer numbers but rather of thousands of well-trained women scientists. Once you have the education, the opportunities will open for you. Do not be afraid of change; if you reach the top in one company, do some more studying and change your position. Companies will not like it, but the age in which a fixed person for a fixed job seemed to be a blessing has passed, and immobility is now a detriment. Ideas and products are conceived, researched, designed and implemented, marketed and outmoded in five to ten years. When you have reached the top echelon of a company and it will not make you president, go into business for yourself. In all of this the ingredients required are good education, strong motivation, and most important, long, hard work.

We have been told that women work 38 hours a week while men work 43. That is easy to cure. You work 50 or 60, or, as I have, 70 or 80.

Now a word on discrimination. I have been in business for almost 19 years, and from my experience I have found that, rather than discrimination, it is a shyness and almost a reaction of surprise on the part of a man when a woman walks into his office. For the past 20, 50 or 100 years, the visitor has worn a man's suit, and suddenly in I come, or in you come. But if you know your product and you know your work and you work hard, you are going to succeed.

It has been suggested that homemakers are great boosters of career women. On the contrary, it has been my experience that the executive secretary to the president is not a booster of the professional woman. Getting past the secretary to see the president is a problem for all business people, but particularly for women. In other respects too, women are their own worst enemy. They sometimes spend their energy trying to figure out what the men are thinking when they would do better to set up a target and go after it. They could help each other, but how many women, in need of a serious operation, would choose a woman doctor? Or if they were involved in a court case, would engage a woman lawyer? How many women gave any serious thought to Margaret Chase Smith's running for president of the United States? I do not say women should choose a woman lawyer or doctor or engineer just because she happens to be a woman, but neither should we not use her just because she happens to be a woman.

Your generation can start to make engineering a woman's field, first of all, by working at it, but you are not going to be able to do it without a goal. After you marry and raise a family, you must encourage your daughters along those lines. And you must also, as Mrs. Kerby-Miller has mentioned, insist that the high school teachers do likewise.

Now a word about marriage. It is here to stay. You can

always reenter your field regardless of your age if you take the trouble to reprepare yourself. Just bear in mind that the late Dr. Sarah Jordan, one of the most famous internists in the world, did not start her medical career until she was in her forties and her children were already married. I believe very strongly that we all have but one obligation in this world, and that is to use our God-given ability to the utmost. Do this and you will have peace of mind and contentment whether it is in marriage or in science or as the first woman president of the United States.

WOMEN ENGINEERS IN INDUSTRY

W. Scott Hill

Though I am here representing industry broadly, because industry includes hundreds of thousands of positions, I can do little more than indicate how industry feels about the employment of women engineers. Actually, these comments relate more to the electrical manufacturing segment of industry, or perhaps only to my own observations in the General Electric Company.

Statistically there are roughly 30,000,000 women working in the United States today. Of these, nearly 8,000 women are employed in engineering and another 15,000 in the natural sciences. This is an effective reply to the question of whether women can or should hold positions in the technical field; the employment figures show that they do.

A brief historical comment may be in order. In 1924, which was 40 years ago, the General Electric Company had a total of 2 women engineers. Incidentally both these women had studied at M.I.T. During the intervening 40 years the number of female technically trained college graduates employed in our company has grown to over 360, which represents something more than 1 per cent of our total number of technically trained college graduates. A meeting to discuss the place of American women in the scientific and engineering world would obviously have been inconceivable 40 or even 30 years ago. I doubt if today's college students can realize the changes in attitudes towards the employment of women that have come about, particularly since the Second World War.

You women are concerned about the problems of your own future, so let us get down to some specific data on this subject. Will you be interviewed or will companies be willing to interview you on campus? From my own observation of other companies and speaking for my own company, I would say, very definitely, yes. As long as I can recall, we have interviewed women on our college schedules. Occasionally a woman is a member of our interviewing team and, although I cannot speak for the women who so serve, I can say that the men on the team definitely enjoy having a woman come in to be interviewed. Though the looks of the applicant may not escape their notice, there is a more important reason for their attention. A college is a selecting and screening operation in itself, and a very fine one. For a woman to complete a program and earn a degree in engineering or science takes more persistence, I think, than is required of a man, and thus there is a double screening. Consequently, the interviewer is usually keen to find out as much as possible about a woman's abilities and where he could fit her into his organization. I think there is no question but that you will be welcome when you come in for an interview.

It may still be true that not all companies are willing to interview women. But 60% or more of the companies have indicated that they do hire women in the technical fields, and these companies probably include at least 600,000 technical jobs that are now held by men. As has often been said, there is no insurmountable problem about finding a position provided you are qualified, so you need not be too concerned about the other 40% of industries who may feel that their positions are not well adapted to careers for women.

How many women are hired? Let me give G.E.'s own figures as some indication. It is true that G.E. is a large company. It employs about 26,000 technical people counting the physical scientists, mathematicians, and engineers. In 1963 about 130 women came in to talk with us, and in 1964, 140. Of these we hired 23 in 1963 and 19 in 1964. This difference between numbers interviewed and hired is not unusual. After sorting out those who were interested in our work and who interested us, we made offers to 31 in June 1964. Incidentally, the ratio of final acceptance for women was higher than for men.

Where in the organization are women likely to work? About three-quarters of the women who come into an industrial company wind up in the laboratory, working on development or design, or in computers. The other quarter probably go into one form or another of manufacturing, some into consulting, and a few into sales. Incidentally, sales may be a woman's field in retail merchandizing, but it is not yet one in heavy industry.

What about some of the jobs that women go into? To take a random sample, G.E. has women working in celestial mechanics doing trajectory problems, in jet engine design on production tests for antiaircraft gun sights, and as heat-transfer analysts. Several women have the title of Manager in Advanced Computer Applications, and others work on scientific programming, electronic systems, and, of course, in chemistry and physics in our research laboratories.

In many positions involving design, engineers may make field trips to customer locations when the application of their work is under discussion or if field problems develop. Although women engineers were viewed as a novelty at first, they are now accepted on such trips.

We have had several young women successfully complete the advanced education programs of our company, which takes three years. Of the first two, one finished the Electronics "C" Course at Syracuse, the other, the Applied Mechanics "C" Course at Cincinnati.

Another way to appraise performance is to look at honors that have come to these women. Some of our women engineers have been chairmen of their local technical societies, the ASME, for example. Many have written books. A great many of them teach classes.

Or you may ask, how much are they paid? This question has no fixed answer. We can say that, in general, starting salaries are comparable to those of men. Starting salaries are determined by matching abilities and jobs; they vary among men and will vary also for women, depending on their qualifications. There may be more information in the progress they have made. In the upper 30% of the 360 women in our company, some 100 people, the lowest salaries are a little below $10,000 a year. Now salary is not everything, but it is one of the measures that industry, and perhaps the academic world also, puts on people. Women often ask, how far can I go? I know of one top-flight woman who is on a level that would bring her salary to over $19,000. So, whether or not you have a chance to become president of the company, there is still considerable room for salary growth if you have the ability.

A discussion from the industrial standpoint is not complete without some references to the working cycle. When men are hired it is generally on the supposition that, if they make good and if they like the company, they are probably going to remain with us for most of their working life. The average young woman who is hired stays only three or four years. The large majority of those who drop out to raise families do not return, at least, not to engineering jobs. In a rapidly advancing field of technology time away from practice is important. If this is only a year or two, it is not too serious. If it runs to 10 or 15 years, as it often does, a woman is faced with the problem of keeping up to date, unless she accepts consulting assignments on the side. Even so, it may be difficult to pick up where she left off. This may be another reason why the percentage of women in engineering has remained static for the last ten years. When they do come back into the job market, they may select other opportunities that use their technical background, but that do not require them to be the equivalent of the new graduates in the latest technologies.

But let us return to the satisfaction, or glamour if you like, of technical work. Most of us are in engineering or scientific work because of the satisfactions, the enjoyment, and the sense of contribution that we get out of our work. So I suggest that the measure we apply should not be limited to salary or title or size of company. I think satisfaction is a good term.

When you return to your colleges from this meeting and your associates ask, what are the real facts about jobs in science and engineering, I think you can act as good ambassadors on this subject of opportunities for women, because the opportunities are here and they will be increasing. The number of technical positions available to women has increased enormously in the last 40 years; it can be expected to continue to increase during the next 40 years of your working careers. At the same time, and to be honest about it, there are some difficulties. But, as in most problem situations, they can be overcome.

When women successfully complete an engineering education, they find many opportunities. Those who stay with the field and have ability can reach highly responsible positions. One of our engineering managers made a remark that is a fitting conclusion. He said, "I hire brains, not gender."

RETRAINING FOR EMPLOYMENT

Eleanor Webster

Much of what has been said at this conference is relevant to any career to which women make a professional commitment, but the problems faced by the woman in science are further complicated by the fact that creative science is a continuing, progressive enterprise whose rate of growth is unbelievably rapid and whose direction of growth is often unpredictable. Those of us in teaching are constantly aware of this. Topics that we first encountered as senior science majors or as graduate students 10 or 15 years ago are routinely taught to freshmen. As a result, some experts have maintained that this exponential growth makes it unrealistic to attempt retraining in science. It is true that most women (and most men for that matter) whose professional careers in science have been interrupted for any length of time find it almost impossible to reenter the kind of creative research that changes fundamental scientific ideas or wins Nobel Prizes. It *is* possible, however, to retrain for employment that is rewarding, satisfying, and genuinely significant.

Lately colleges and universities all over the country have been expanding their extension offerings or inaugurating continuing education programs for adult women. Some businesses and industries have given on-the-job retraining for special kinds of employment. By and large, however, there have been few efforts to focus particularly on the needs of the woman originally trained in science or engineering.

We are starting an experiment at Wellesley this year to see if women who have been away from their undergraduate study of chemistry for five to twenty years can successfully complete a two-year half-time program leading to the master's degree and can return to productive work in chemistry. Since our first group of five participants is just now beginning the fifth week of classes, our modest experiment is far from complete, but I *can* say that the five have survived the first four weeks and are still enthusiastic.

The response to brief announcements of this program was immediate and gratifying — there *was* an interested audience. There were letters or telephone inquiries from more than a hundred and twenty women, most of whom had majored in science and were eager to retrain for employment. With National Science Foundation support we were able to offer free tuition and modest stipends to help cover some of the costs of child care, transportation, books, and so on. There were surprisingly few who were altogether ineligible, though there *were* inquiries from two men and one woman who had not studied any science; she said to me, "I know I'd be excellent at research, I simply love to look things up!" In evaluating applications we looked carefully at the amount of undergraduate chemistry, mathematics, and physics (generally much less of the latter two for a degree in 1944 than in 1964), and at the quality of the record, but we placed more emphasis on evidence since college of continued interest and involvement in chemistry, however unsystematic or informal. We tried in personal interviews to evaluate motivation and the degree to which these women recognized realistically the demands of such a program.

Whom did we choose? Our participants completed their undergraduate majors 6, 8, 14, 15, and 19 years ago. Even the youngest, who has no children and who has been working full time as a laboratory assistant in biochemistry, is out of date — obviously the others are more so. Over the summer all were required to do independent study — to review calculus and the chemistry now taught in the first two years of college. During the school year, each of them is carrying two upper-level courses for credit, and each one is auditing a third course in which she is expected to take quizzes and exams. Some of them are sitting in on another course — one in which they are especially interested or in which they wish further review. During the second year, in addition to two courses for credit, each of them will teach a laboratory section. Having to teach is a kind of learning in itself — sometimes the most effective kind. Although the participants have no commitment to Wellesley or to the NSF to go into teaching, it is certainly our hope that some will wish to do so.

From talking with many interested women, we received informal confirmation of some of the assumptions we had made in designing our plan. Despite a wealth of part-time study opportunities for the educated woman in the Boston area (Radcliffe's *The Next Step*[1] devotes about 40 pages to them), there are difficulties in making arrangements for the kind of upper-level work in chemistry and related fields

[1] Published in 1964 by The Radcliffe Institute for Independent Study, Cambridge, Mass.

needed for retraining. For the older woman who wishes part-time study, commuting into Boston, often for evening classes, may require an inordinate expenditure of time and money. Although this kind of intermittent study is certainly useful, we believe that effective retraining for employment must usually be both more concentrated and more coherent.

Those of us who are giving full time to science find it next to impossible to keep up to date — how much more difficult for the woman whose scientific career must be interrupted! Can she do anything, other than formal study, to keep in touch? I think so, if she can develop a degree of expertness in some special field of interest, and if she will make a serious commitment to it. If she is determined, she can keep informed by reading scientific journals, review articles, and monographs; with even a limited budget she can obtain the best of the new paperback books written to supplement textbooks. She can certainly follow general trends in such magazines as *Science, Nature, Physics Today, The Journal of Chemical Education,* and the *Scientific American.* Of course, for an experimental scientist, reading by one's self rather than working with colleagues is clearly an inadequate solution, although it is certainly better than none.

What do our participants expect from our retraining program? Can it make possible employment in chemistry? We believe so, of course, or we should not be conducting our experiment. For women who can manage only part-time work, teaching and technical literature (for example, editing, abstracting, reviewing) seem to offer an excellent combination of flexibility, responsibility, and scope for independent ingenuity. Laboratory work that is challenging and stimulating is more difficult to arrange for on a part-time basis. (I might add parenthetically that, although our participants are unanimous in their view that 5 to 20 years in the kitchen are no preparation for a deft, efficient, and elegant initial afternoon in the laboratory, their skill is returning rapidly.) Since experimental research at its best is all-absorbing, and hence time-consuming, it seems to offer a more suitable career for the woman ready to work full time.

In conclusion, I should like to cite what seems to me the best evidence we have so far that "the mature woman . . . can retrain, can find interesting work, and can enjoy both her job and her home."[1] Since 1961 almost two hundred women (and, incidentally, a couple of men) have had a semester or more of work in the Mathematics Retraining Program at Rutgers. Last spring the tally showed that 54 of them held jobs attributable to their retraining, over half of them in teaching, 60 were continuing in the program, and 30 had started on work toward a master's degree. The success of the Rutgers program suggests that there are certain advantages in designing course work to meet the particular needs of particular audiences (and class schedules at convenient hours for commuting students with young children). However, an important feature of our experiment at Wellesley is to find out whether we can retrain within the framework of our regular course offerings, and we hope that other colleges and universities will be encouraged to try to develop other coherent part-time study opportunities in science.

[1] *Notes and Comments from the Mathematical Retraining Program.* Rutgers — The State University, New Brunswick, New Jersey, April 1964.

GOVERNMENT INTEREST IN THE EMPLOYMENT OF WOMEN

ROBERT F. MELLO

The federal government's interest in womanpower has been receiving considerable publicity in the recent past. One of your neighbors, Radcliffe College, has graciously furnished their President, Dr. Mary Bunting, in support of this interest and need.

As director of College Relations and Recruitment for the U.S. Civil Service Commission I have been directed to assure that the government's national recruiting efforts include an aggressive program to attract qualified women to the challenging jobs we have to offer. This, of course, includes women in the sciences and engineering.

There are many reasons for this emphasis, the major one being your government's vital need for high-quality talent, regardless of race, color, creed — or sex. Women have been making and will continue to make a major contribution to the significant programs being pursued by the government and are personally engaged in the solution of problems of international impact and significance. More — many more — are needed if we are to maintain our leadership in the world of tomorrow, particularly in the sciences and engineering.

My interest in this topic is considerably different today from what it was not long ago. Prior to my national responsibility for college relations and recruitment for the federal government, I was more directly concerned with the use of scientific talent in an important research program. This might serve as a prelude to the situation as it is today.

For six and one-half years before my appointment to the Civil Service Commission, I served as Director of Personnel for the Army Ordnance Missile Command. The Command had, and still has, a responsibility for basic and applied research and the development of prototype hardware.

We hired hundreds of scientists and engineers, some of whom were women. Unfortunately, too few of them were, in spite of our aggressive efforts to reach them in our on- and off-campus recruiting.

I have these observations to make about the women we did employ in entrance-level positions.

They were hired at the same entrance level as the men, and they progressed to the journeyman level at the same prescribed intervals — if they stayed as long as that. Many left for family reasons, mostly marriage and related reasons, such as pregnancy, husband's moving, etc.

The women we employed in research and laboratory positions did excellent work. In relationship to the number of women employed, they progressed to supervisory levels at the same ratio as did the men. They were equally effective.

We encountered difficulty when women were used on

field problems, or in negotiations or inspection of work being performed by private contractors or other government agencies.

Most of the field problems involved technical work on actual missile hardware in field situations. Much of this was in concert with their male counterparts. Although the women were capable, they did not contribute as much as men did in the same situation. The reason can be attributed partly to prejudice on the part of the supervisors, partly to the nature of the problem, and partly to the fact that their presence as a woman among several men had an impact that hampered their potential contribution. Whatever the reason, it was a fact.

In negotiations with our private contractors and inspection of contract activities, women were only marginally successful. They were not accepted as the men were, and their professional ability had little to do with it.

Why this prejudice? Why should women be placed only in certain positions where they can make only a marginal or incomplete contribution, and excluded from other positions where their contribution could be of greater value, and is perhaps more vitally needed? History, and fairly recent history at that, provides part of the answer.

Ever since 1870 there has been a law which has been interpreted as giving federal department heads the authority to hire women "if they wished," or only men. This meant that, if a federal appointing officer asked the Civil Service Commission to send him the names of *men only* from their lists of eligible applicants for any kind of position, the Commission had no choice but to do so. The ruling thus gave legal sanction to a discriminatory practice that had gone on all along, conferring upon it a degree of respectability that other forms of discrimination did not have.

Now it is equally true that this interpretation gave agency heads the right to ask for "*women* only" to fill the positions of nurse, stenographer, typist, or charwoman — which they did. But that is a pretty unimportant right when you consider that women were virtually the only applicants for those jobs anyway. Much more important is the fact that "men only, please" became the order of the day for the vast majority of jobs above the lowest third of the salary scale — for the professional, administrative, scientific, and technical jobs.

To shorten a rather long story, the contribution of women during World War II, the recommendations of the Commission on the Status of Women, and a decision of the Attorney General reversed the interpretation and administration of this law. Now the Civil Service Commission requires that all appointments be made without regard to sex, unless specific exceptions are granted — and these are few and far between.

One of the most interesting chapters in this curious story, however, took place before the legal question was decided. Immediately after the Commission on the Status of Women was established, Chairman John W. Macy of the Civil Service Commission took the preliminary step of directing federal appointing officers to include specific reasons with any request that asked for eligible applicants of one sex only. Although the Civil Service Commission could not at that time legally overrule the request of the appointing officer, it could require him to submit reasons. This had not been done before.

The results were immediate, dramatic, and very revealing: requests specifying sex suddenly dropped to *less than 1 per cent* of the total. It seems very clear that the practice of requesting men for most jobs was largely habit, and that when appointing officers had to stop and think about it they realized that there was no real reason in most cases.

Today we have evidence that prejudice is being reduced.

The Federal Woman's Award was established in 1960 to turn the spotlight of public attention on the achievements of government career women. This award is conferred each year on six women who have demonstrated outstanding ability and achievement in executive, professional, scientific, or technical positions. Candidates for the award are nominated by the heads of the government agencies in which they are employed, and the winners are selected by an independent panel of judges from outside the government. Criteria for nomination are very high, but there is never any shortage of nominees.

The 24 women who have received the award so far include an astrophysicist, two attorneys, an aviation expert, a chemist, two research scientists, an economist-statistician, four executives, three Foreign Service officers, a geologist, a pathologist in cancer research, a director of personnel, a physician who is also a hospital administrator, a prison warden, a radiological physicist, two space scientists, and a transportation economist.

It is obvious that women working for the government today and in the recent past have by no means been limited to careers in the traditional "women's occupations."

Let me provide a larger picture, statistically, of women in government, and narrow this down to those in the sciences and engineering.

Of the 600,000 women now working for the federal government, about 10 per cent are in professional occupations — those requiring a prescribed course of study resulting in a degree. About 10 per cent of these are in the sciences and engineering. We can all agree that, compared with the contribution being made by women in other nations, this is not a very impressive statistic.

As to monetary rewards, our statistics show that the average salary for women in the federal government is at about the GS-4 grade level (approximately $4,500 per year), and for men at the GS-9 grade level (approximately $7,300 per year). However, in the sciences and engineering 25 per cent of women are earning salaries in excess of $10,000 per year, and in engineering over 40 per cent are in this bracket. The average salaries are about the same for women as they are for men.

We would like to have more women with talent in the sciences and engineering to participate in federal programs and demonstrate that the "for men only" sign is inappropriate. At the entrance levels and above, there are opportunities unlimited for those who can qualify.

The two sources for this talent are obvious: the future graduating classes from the many fine schools represented here today and the alumnae of these schools. I see no problems in using talent from either source—with one exception.

I am constantly reminded that there are women with degrees in the sciences and engineering who have now raised their family and are ready to get back into the swim of technology. This is an excellent source of talent, but it is not an easy one to use, particularly in our technical research programs. The changes that have taken place since they received their degree prevent women from making the contribution they desire: not any contribution but a full professional one. This would be the same for a man who had left his profession and had not kept abreast of the changes in his professional discipline.

Science has changed so rapidly that many of the occupational titles we use today — such as cybernetics and cryogenics — were practically unknown words a generation ago.

The change is so rapid, in fact, that many of our doctors of philosophy find it necessary to go back to school periodically to catch up on new knowledge that has been developed since they were graduated. Certainly this is true for the scientist.

I heard it said recently that the half-life of a physicist today is 10 years — meaning that, 10 years after graduation, half the knowledge a physicist acquired in college has become obsolete.

Now we come to the question: what can be done to improve the opportunities for women in the sciences and engineering?

First, there is no doubt about the need. In the federal government there are more opportunities than there are scientists and engineers, regardless of their sex. If the talent is available, it will be used. I am sure my industrial associates will voice the same opinion. We need more scientists and engineers than there are now in the schools, and we need more — many many more — talented high school students to take an interest in these professions to assure that the needs of tomorrow will be satisfied.

Encouragement from those who can demonstrate this need — for instance, the young women scientists of today — can do much toward improving this situation. Tours, science fairs, scholarship support, lectures, all these will help, but encouragement from those who know is absolutely essential. Presentations before student groups, counselors, PTA, and public groups, by women in the sciences and engineering will do much toward motivating our youth, as well as those who suggest direction to them.

As to reducing prejudice, this is now taking place, and the federal government is determined to eliminate it as rapidly as possible. As our technology advances and our needs for manpower (and womanpower) increase, prejudice will move further into the background toward oblivion. Demonstrated ability is the best answer to prejudice, and the opportunities are available.

For the women who are not up to date in their professions, there should be refresher courses available to avoid wasting this resource. Where this is not possible, an alternate contribution should be considered. Technical writing, technical assistance to a scientist or engineer, translation of scientific papers if one has the skill, management positions in support of technical programs, and a variety of other possibilities come to mind. The academic skill is useful, but perhaps some consideration should be given to a compromise when the full skill is not usable. It is the contribution that is of utmost importance.

A career in science or engineering is not necessarily incompatible with raising a family. However, if it is necessary for you to make a choice between raising a family and keeping current in your profession, then my advice is: choose the family. If the family becomes obsolete, we can anticipate problems that will reach far beyond those being considered today.

In conclusion, let me repeat some advice that was given at a meeting for women in science some years ago in Washington by one of your contemporaries, Ethaline Cortelyou.

> Be a woman and be glad of it. Lipsticks and slipsticks are entirely compatible, and a pretty hat does not mean the head under it is empty.

To that I can only add *Amen!*

PART IV

Closing the Gap

CLOSING THE GAP

LILLIAN M. GILBRETH

CONCLUDING REMARKS

ERIK H. ERIKSON

CLOSING THE GAP

LILLIAN M. GILBRETH

As I started to plan this talk, I was not quite sure what "closing the gap" meant. In fact, I did not quite know what "gap" was to be closed. Then, all of a sudden, I had a brain wave and I thought: "Well, why not consider this thing from the point of view of engineering and science?"

Let us see what our past has to tell us about closing gaps, or more especially, about finding answers to problems. From their earliest history, engineers and scientists have been concerned with problems. I am going to consider that part of their work called "management." First, I would like to look back into history to find out what experience in "closing the gap" engineering and science has to offer.

It seems to me, the first thing they offer us is a code of ethics. It is a very simple code, easy to say but not nearly so easy to live up to. It says our job is "to utilize the resources of nature and of human nature for the benefit of mankind." (I think in the beginning it just said "the resources of nature" but some felt that this left people out of the picture, so they added the words "human nature.") You will note in the first place that the code says we are going to "utilize" resources. Of course, if we are going to utilize them we first have to know what they are and where they are. Then we must think about how to utilize them, how to take an idea that some scientist has creatively formulated and put it into useful shape. This too is a creative experience, a "closing of the gap," for when we take ideas, perhaps originated by others, and work with them and organize them and put them into actual use — by you and me and people in industry all over the world — we have utilized resources, both of nature and of human nature. In the wide world today this is one of the most exciting processes of development. People of all countries, as they learn more about engineering and science, are discovering for themselves that they have resources they never even knew about. This brings us to another point: we should remember that not only must we utilize resources, but we must also be sure that we do not waste them. I want to make that point as strong as I can.

The late President Hoover, during his administration, asked our engineers to make a study of natural resources. The report they turned in proved to be on the elimination of waste. It is very interesting. It deals almost entirely with waste in production. If you were to take it off the shelf and read it now, you would see that our waste today is even greater than it was then. In the mid 1960's we do not need to stress the point that waste is tremendous, not only in production, but in the act of taking care of things and in using them properly. We know what happens when people from other countries come here and talk to us. If we really get close enough to them, and they are willing to tell us what they think about our country as compared with their own, we find that they are shocked by our waste. Unfortunately, as they reach America by ship, train or plane, they invariably go past junk heaps of what seem to have been automobiles and farm machinery, just moldering away—equipment that would have been such a wonderful asset and help to them. I remember a group coming to one of the New York universities for a conference. We asked them what aspect of all they had seen impressed them most. They were terribly shocked because they thought we were so wasteful with clothing. They bought their clothing for durability, and that was the chief thing they thought of. Imagine how our manufacturers would complain if *we* thought only of durability! But you can imagine equally well how a country that has a great lack of clothing would feel about our style consciousness, our response to Madison Avenue advertising. There certainly is a tremendous waste in that field.

More than any other, however, I think I notice our waste in food, and I wish so often that we could return to the old custom of the family and the club, where things were passed and one asked for what one wanted. I do not want to overstress the point, but I think the aspect of utilizing resources properly, and seeing that they are not wasted, demands a great deal of creative activity.

In the early days of engineering, not much emphasis was put on the resources of human nature, but in the years since then the field of management has taken a major part in developing them. The pioneers of management, at the beginning of the century, were mechanical engineers. They were extremely interested in the resources of nature. They were all involved in manufacturing and they thought of engineers as people who found and used natural resources. They were also interested in people, but they did not have the resources of so-called social sciences that you and I have today. In reading about these pioneers, we must keep it plainly in mind that, when these people began to use the resources of human nature, they lacked the background of research and utilization of its findings that we have today.

Today, of course, there are foundations for work in psychiatry which have developed and applied their research in such interesting ways! They made a major contribution to the field of management when they simplified their vocabulary in order to report their experience in terms any layman with a real interest in psychiatry could understand.

Think of the courses that are now given for top management. Staff members work as personnel people or workers in different industries. They learn firsthand what the experience of the worker is. Then they can return to their own work with a much better knowledge of the resources of their industry.

In addition to the benefits of social science, we also have the help of the scientific method. Anyone who has had experience with the scientific method knows that it is impossible to overestimate its importance. In management it was developed through the work of those pioneers who were mechanical engineers. They too, like the psychiatrists, had the courage and the foresight to simplify their language. Perhaps you remember Rudyard Kipling's little quatrain from *The Elephant's Child:*

> "I keep six honest serving men
> They taught me all I knew
> Their names are What and Why and When
> And How and Where and Who." [1]

Of course, he might as well have said "serving women," but I suppose that would have spoiled the little rhyme. At any

[1] Reprinted by permission of Mrs. George Bambridge, Doubleday and Company, Inc., and A. P. Watt and Son.

rate, he expresses an idea congenial to people in the management field, that we must always be asking questions.

The growth of the field of management has proved the importance of asking questions. I think it began with the *what* of the situation: "*What* are we doing?" During the first World War the government got out a dictionary of occupational titles. The reaction to it was just what the writers had expected. People wrote in by the hundreds — thousands, perhaps — and said, "That is not the way such and such a job should be done," and "It is not a description of that job." Whereupon, the government very candidly wrote back and said, "Would you kindly sit down and write the job description in the way it should have been written." When the material had all come in, they got out a new edition.

In thinking about different jobs from the human point of view, we naturally thought about the *who* as the management field developed. "*Who* should do it?" And then, "*Where* should it be done?" "*When* should it be done?" Then, tremendous emphasis was placed on "*How* should it be done?" Those, like my husband and others in his field, thought about the expenditure of time and energy. They thought about how one could increase skills and how these additional skills could be transferred to education and training programs. "American know-how" became a sort of praise during the war, and in peacetime described what our men did in creatively utilizing what was at hand, in making-do with whatever they had, and in remaking methods to get the most out of the time and energy spent.

Now we are at the point where we feel that *Why* is the important question "*Why* do we do this?" In many cases it has led us to call in an outside group to work closely with us, to try to help us explain the *why*. One of our jobs from the very beginning, in science and engineering, has been to set down, just as plainly as we possibly could, the standards that should be met. To do that we needed to have the method clearly outlined and to state in exact terms just what the problem was. Now, the problem is not always what it appears to be. Very often we may think that the problem is a mechanical one, only to find, as we go on to solve it, that it is not a mechanical problem at all, but rather one in human relations. Gradually the human relations specialists of every type have come in to work with the engineers so that now we have regular cooperation between those who understand the resources of human nature and those who know about the resources of nature. So you see, in management today the difficulty of stating problems and solving problems is being simplified.

When there is a problem, the first job is to find out what the problem *really* is. You have to go below all the surface indications, and psychiatrists help us enormously with this process. When business men go to a course in management they are asked on the first day to present a problem. Often one of them will say, "Well, I have heard about somebody who had a certain problem, and I think this is also a problem in my shop." As you go on talking, you find out that this particular problem is not the one that is bothering him — although he does have a shop problem. First you try to find out if the workers brought the problem to the shop with them, or if it was one that originated in the shop. As you go on talking you get more and more clues. You hear about this man and that man, and so and so, and finally your client will say, "Well, frankly, I guess it is my own problem I am talking about." So often, when you try to get down to fundamentals, you end up with something that is your own individual problem, or one in which you are in some way intimately involved. That is why you must first find the *real* problem and state it clearly before you begin to look for your resources. Then you try to find the resources and evaluate what they have to offer.

Where do we find these problems we have been talking about? Management says they arise in any place where work is being done, no matter where it is. Let us stress "work" at this point, because life-long learning and the will to work are extremely important in any situation. If you are a scientist or an engineer and you have the will to work, you have a tremendous asset in everything you do.

I like to think that there are five main areas of work that call for good management and I should like to consider them with you. The first one has to do with the much-neglected area of managing oneself. It is tremendously important. I have had the good fortune in my life (and I am now at the stage where I count my age in decades and not in years) to work for many top executives who could manage everything and everybody, but had never really learned to manage themselves. When you went in you would find that the whole organization knew by the grapevine (and you know how effective the grapevine is) exactly when the top executive was getting ready for a tantrum. That is what it really was, just a tantrum. They would say to me, "He wants you to go in, but you had better be very careful, because we think he is just going to blow off steam." Well, I went in — and he did. You would just have to sit there peacefully and watch the volcano explode. After the explosion, very often there was a wonderful calm. Then you were all prepared for him to say, all of a sudden, "Do you have something on your mind?" and you would say, "Yes, sir, do you think we could appropriately . . . ?" and in the most benevolent tone he would say, "Anything you want will be perfectly all right." Then you would just reiterate a little bit, outlining what it was you wanted.

I speak very feelingly and personally to you about managing oneself. When I was a child, everybody believed that if you had red hair you had a hot temper (I mean natural red hair, not dyed red hair). If you had a hot temper it was a great calamity. Your family felt very sorry for you. They would advise you to go to a quiet room and think over your sins, potential and committed, and so on. Well, you fortunate young things, we have progressed since then. Today we feel that a hot temper is an asset. Anything that gives you drive, anything that keeps you on your feet and keeps you going, we admire. We feel sorry for the people who physically, mentally, emotionally—or all three—do not have much temperament. We feel that we should encourage our young people to have just as much drive and energy as they can. Of course there is one little detail: you are supposed to act constructively and not destructively, and that is not always possible. However, it is a very great comfort, I am sure, to have the psychiatrist, and others who study us, tell us that temper is an inborn drive to work. It is the will to work that gets us through and that pledges us physically, mentally, and emotionally, to the thing we are doing. We should all feel obligated to see that our young people, all over the world, have that sort of drive.

The second field that I think we should discuss is the home and the family. Too many people underestimate the importance of the home and family. The woman who is the homemaker is the one who most often belittles her importance. If you say to her, "And what do you do in your work?" she is apt to say in a very dejected tone of voice, "Oh, I am only a homemaker." Of course, if you want to downgrade yourself and feel that homemaking is not a very aspiring occupation, and that it does not command general interest or respect, that is your fault. But that is a great mistake, because the quality of your homemaking not only determines what happens within the home and family, but it affects all contacts and all jobs and everything that family members do. Furthermore, it extends to all those who come in and out of your home, to neighbors and friends and everyone who belongs to the same organizations that family members do.

Now I think we all feel that the home and the family are successful if the housekeeping is good and the family relations are happy. Many people think that the first is of no importance and that the second is all-important, but I have a feeling that the housekeeping should at least be perfectly acceptable to the family and to those nearby.

If you leave your home happy and rested and the traffic does not destroy you, physically or otherwise, before you get to the job, you are bound to be an asset to your group. When I am working on a job and see men and women of this type coming in, I know that, even when the problems are most difficult, I shall find some steadiness, some support, for I shall be working with a group who can quickly establish teamwork and will understand and be willing to work for a goal. But if, on the other hand, the group comes from families that are unhappy for one reason or another, my attempt to make their industrial life happy and to encourage them to share in partnerships all along the line is quite apt to fail. I am apt to be very much let down and especially disappointed when something I thought was going to give a great deal of pleasure just does not do so, for I feel there is something wrong with me. Something may be wrong with the job, something may be wrong with the industry; yet very often the job and the industry are running smoothly and the problem is brought in by the group that comes from unhappy homes.

On the other hand, I feel strongly that the work places of the community — the schools, factories, businesses — should endeavor to return people to their homes at the end of the day in a happy frame of mind. Of course it takes a little while for almost all of us to adjust to the different situation when we arrive at home. If we have been driving hard all day, trying to put things through, and have really used up a lot of energy, our nerves are perhaps on edge. Even the most loving wife and children coming out and hauling you to pieces — "Why don't you cooperate?" or "Why don't you drop that foolish business?" — can be just plain hard to take. You have to allow a little time for adjustment. I never understood that until I went to work myself, and I did not work outside the home regularly until after my husband died, because he brought work home to me and I fitted it in with my homemaking responsibilities.

If there were time, I would tell you about a project that I was part of for two years, in which we talked to the wives of executives while the men were at meetings. It was very interesting, because the wives took a little time to unwind, but when they did they became so much interested that you could not break up the meetings. The husbands' meetings would end and the men would all come and peek in the door to see what their wives were doing and thinking about. We found that, by and large, the man who was not hurried when he came home was the happiest. One wife who had no help, and you know most of us do not have any these days, would go on cooking dinner when her husband came home. She had a rocker in the kitchen, with his slippers, the newspaper and two or three other things at hand. It was right near the stove and she just quietly went about her work while he got himself comfortable. Then he was apt to say, "Would you like to know what happened today?" I could go on indefinitely, but that must be all of that.

It is important for us to appreciate the importance of the citizen's job in the community. We underestimate the importance of citizen activities. They ought to start when we are children. I love to see the boys with the white strap managing traffic. The other day I went by a crossroads near a school, and the boys who had been assigned, one to each corner, were all sort of scuffling with each other, having a wonderful time, while an obedient line of cars waited until they calmed down and got ready to direct the traffic. Just the same, I felt that it was a wonderful project. And so is the way they train people now — at least they do in my town and I think in most small towns — not only to respect, but also to fraternize with, the fireman and the policeman. We really do not try hard enough to utilize all the resources within community service. We should begin to appreciate again the importance of the citizen's job in the community.

The volunteer job, too, is a tremendously vital part of our lives. I feel very proud that the engineers and the management people have take on so much of this sort of thing. You find them working in hospitals, in libraries, on the farm, going into the Peace Corps, and so forth and so on. Very often, quite to their surprise, they are developing new opportunities for trained people in their field. So now we are encouraging young men and women to take on volunteer work in hospitals and other places in order that the techniques that have been tried and tested in engineering and industrial engineering may be carried over into these various fields, for it is sometimes through volunteer work that new professional areas are gradually opened up. Then subsequently people are trained to give their whole time to these new types of work.

Finally, there is the job that is so important to you and to all of us. I mean our career, whatever it may be.

I am really not much worried about opportunities for women. I am much more concerned about opportunities for *people.*

Automation is a far more serious thing than most of us realize. From the day that we simplified the first work method, back in the pioneer days, I have worried about what would happen to the people we had dispensed with. Every time you simplify a work method, you save time and energy, but you also create a problem. I think we should have recognized much sooner what automation would do. I think perhaps we did recognize what it could do about lifting the burden of drudgery and the burden of work, about saving time and energy, and so on. It is a wonderful gift, provided we are ready to use it wisely but, of course, not everybody appreciates the predicament it imposes upon us. Now suppose you are in an industry in which you have to discontinue the jobs of a certain number of men who have run some particular machines. It is very difficult to place them in other positions. You may say, "Well, if they can run these industrial machines, they can probably run business machines." And so they can, but they will first have to be educated, they will have to be trained before they can change jobs. A man who has been doing an industrial job down in the shop — a "blue collar" job — and is moved to another type of work not only has to learn the techniques of the new job, but may also find himself working with a different group of people. He may have to change his vocabulary and the kind of clothes he wears on the job. He may even have to move to a different neighborhood.

We shall face many problems in the future that will demand that careful thought be given to the ways in which changes are made. Many of these changes will be worldwide, but through education and training they can be accomplished. Changes will need to be made, not only in schools and colleges, but in our individual programs for life-long learning.

It seems to me that very often we Americans assume that we know everything and have tried everything, and that we are automatically ahead of all the rest of the world. World leadership means teaching, that is true, but it also means life-long learning. I greatly fear that, when people from other countries come to us, we often take the attitude that we are doing all the teaching and all the giving, and that they are doing all the taking, all the learning. We forget all too easily that there is not a country that does not have something to give and from which we cannot learn. We are doing fairly well in some areas, and some of the time, but there are countries that surpass us in many important respects. There are countries where there are no unhappy old people, where nobody is made to feel unwanted, everybody is made to feel that there is a specific job for him to do. This is true in his home and it is true in his work. In our country I think we certainly try to be kind to our own children — indeed we are perhaps sometimes a little too permissive, a little too kind in the wrong way — but we do not usually extend the same love and kindness to children not our own. However, there are countries where every child is everybody's child. There may not be much food, there may not be much clothing, there may not be much of anything, but the children have whatever there is. There are countries that are not as materialistic as we are, that are more spiritually minded and more articulate about their religion. People in these countries go through the rites of their religion at any time, in any place, with no sense of embarrassment or queer feeling. There are countries where the beautiful means more than it does to most of us, where people are actually willing to sacrifice food for the opportunity to enjoy something that is lovely.

Life-long learning, the willingness to learn from people everywhere, utilization of human and natural resources and a feeling that, after all, it is a blessing to be alive. These are important values for a nation to possess.

It is wonderful to want to give, but I think we are really far too apt to put the emphasis on receiving. I hope in the future no man or woman will ever continually say, "What's in it for me?" or "How much money do I get?" and "What about this, that and the other?" Getting is all very well, but giving is more important than getting.

Whenever one goes into a group with the idea of giving what one can, learning and teaching are both required. You remember what Chaucer said: "First he wrought and afterwards he taught." That is a direct message for us. Let us be sure that we have integrity and recognize that cheerful giving is a thing worth doing. Chaucer also said, "Gladly would we learn and gladly teach."

In our role as women, however, it seems to me that the most important thing is to be able to share, not simply bits and pieces of information, but the warmth of friendly interest in one another's affairs. As Lowell put it,

> "Not what we give but what we share,
> For the gift without the giver is bare."

I love to think about that!

I hope that you find this whole field interesting. I remember a time in Nantucket when one of my girls, quite young, had a date with a young man that she thought was just exactly the last word in dates—and he did not come. She stood by the window, looking and crying, and having a terrible time. I tried to encourage her and finally, I am ashamed to say, I cried. She looked at me with tears rolling down and she said, "Never mind, Mother dear, never mind. It is very sad, but isn't it interesting?"

Well, I hope you all have a continuously happy time, and, if it is not happy at the moment, I certainly hope it will be interesting!

CONCLUDING REMARKS

Erik H. Erikson

It is a great honor to follow Dr. Gilbreth on this rostrum — even in the absolute certainty that thereby one is going to be an anticlimax. I shall not even try to match her address with another one. I can only conclude the proceedings with a few critical remarks (in the sense of critique rather than of criticism) that reflect on what we have heard in the last two days, and yet also look forward to future meetings of this kind.

In doing so, I hope not to appear unmindful of the labor of others — like the relieved young husband who on viewing their newborn in the hospital said to his wife, "That was easy, why not have another one soon?" Rather, in full awareness of the magnificent job done by the organizers of this meeting, I hope to gain some perspective by speaking of future possibilities.

For one thing I would like to have heard more from you, the delegates. Have you not listened a bit too much and said much too little, at least in open meeting? What you have heard came from many backgrounds and many points of view, and this, to be sure, was a refreshing and enlightening start. But I think that the speakers who participated in this symposium did not mean to ask you to believe at first hearing every thesis they advanced. They meant to stimulate you to think about the alternative conclusions one could draw from all this material, in the hope that you would, surely but slowly, come around to their point of view. We must follow up these leads.

Further reasons for visualizing another meeting bring me back to the first session of this one. Dr. Bettelheim, the first speaker, with the modesty that befits the first (and most exposed) speaker, expressed the hope that on another occasion the first speaker would be a woman. I did wonder, as you may have, why the preparatory committee selected Bruno Bettelheim and me to be the first and the last speakers. Not only two men, but two men with psychiatric backgrounds "made in Europe."

There was a time, of course, when meetings of this and similar kinds were introduced or concluded by members of an entirely different profession, whose sense of continuity and purpose was closer to metaphysics than to metapsychology, to the source of all destiny rather than to the dynamics of individual adjustment. Today, however, much of the daily concern with the continuity of individual lives and of the sequence of generations has (as Mrs. Gilbreth also pointed out) shifted to the clinical field, and I assume that Dr. Bettelheim and I were asked to speak in order to reflect your own concern over the often endangered continuity in the professional life of a modern woman.

President Bunting also spoke of the necessity to "maximize continuities" under rapidly changing conditions. I remember a little boy who put this dilemma into classic form. He had asked his mother: "What is going to happen to me when I die?" and she had answered, with the finality born of uncertainty, "Well, your body is going to be buried in the ground and your soul is going to go up to heaven." But he was not satisfied. "Mommy," he said, "I'd rather keep my stuff together." This is the challenging task, even in life on this earth: how in changing conditions to keep your stuff together — to be women and workers, wives and colleagues, mothers and creative beings, and have a sense of continuity. But such a sense has always depended on blueprints that anticipated change, whether they were religious or scientific, fatalistic or forward looking. Today, when planning has become our evolutionary heritage, this means to learn to change *actively*, to help *plan* inescapable change, and also to become *aware*, and probably even self-conscious at times, in regard to what one is doing to oneself and to others. For you are pioneers of a new kind. You are pioneers not only on a new frontier of activity and association, but also on an inner frontier, which includes new responsibilities for changes in yourselves and in others: your men, your children — and, yes, mankind. A certain self-consciousness, then, may not be avoidable; it can, in fact, be creatively used if it is not shirked. Here I would think that in any future symposium you might want to include Dr. Benson Snyder and draw on his experience. He is (as most of you know) the chief psychiatrist here at M.I.T., or what our Harvard Crimson would call "the top shrink." He has concerned himself with the personalities of the budding engineer and scientist and with the particular tensions that go with that kind of work; and Dean Mattfeld and he have no doubt collected insights and suggestions concerning the role of women in these fields. I missed hearing from them and from you concerning the tensions of your work *as perceived by you.*

I must add to the other characteristics that I share with Dr. Bettelheim that of age. Our conceptual ancestry goes back to the days of Freud who studied the psychological tensions of his era, which is, in turn, the past of ours: an era of unlimited human progress based on unrestrained commercial expansion, and an all-powerful middle class. While revolutionizing the science and treatment of severe mental suffering, he also recognized conditions that were part and parcel of the changing history and technology, and the scruples and tensions often befalling the sensitive, the advanced, and some of the successful of his time. Maybe, then, our mandate is to help you keep watch over the changes in our society and the tensions that could befall those aspiring to success in the era to come. But instead of basing our assessments on a passing age, on theories of human nature that we now know undergo change at least to some extent as conditions and eras change, we would rather hope that we will hear more from you. For we need to know better where exactly you need our insights.

A second set of reasons for my wish for further meetings concerns you more exclusively, you the young women delegates. What will you do with all the things that you have heard here? Of course, you will report to your colleagues. And, if I may make a guess, you wonder — but why offer you a prophetic interpretation, when I can tell you of an experience? Not long ago, I talked about womanhood at one of our technical institutes. Afterwards I had a discussion with a number of alert and attractive young women who seemed strangely pensive. I asked them to tell me what they really felt about what I had said in my lecture. They discussed it for a moment among themselves and agreed on this reply: "What you said makes sense — but *how do we tell our boyfriends?*" This problem is so important that a future meeting might well be named "Women *and Men* in Engineering and Science" with an emphasis on what nowadays is called a dialogue of men and women. I have not checked this with your committee, but maybe each delegate should have the privilege and the duty of bringing one man of intimate acquaintance, if necessary with some assistance from the Marines. For it was clear in this two-day meeting that underlying many of the difficulties of women in the fields discussed (whether discrimination in industry or government, in the home or in society) there is always that most basic discrimination and prejudice against themselves that still exists in the minds of women themselves; and that this (now as in all history) is related to the question of how the men will react if women dare to change. Women, in turn, deeply sympathize with the apprehensions on the part of men as to what might happen if women really did take part in all of those activities that men have considered their privilege and their preserve and *from* which most men seek refuge by returning to women. And it is hard to look for refuge in a would-be competitor. In some discussions men otherwise not of a sentimental bent insist so strenuously that children need their mothers at home that one cannot help wondering if it is not the husband himself who is the needy person — the tired husband who wants a ravishing companion free of all connotations of the office and the lab.

But there is a more pertinent explanation for his resistance to a change in the image of the woman: a clear elaboration of sexual types is always essential for the polarization of the sexes in sexual life and in their respective identity formation. For this and many other reasons, there is even a possibility that as the number of competitive women in these fields increases, there may well be something of a male "backlash." I have found among the most educated, the most attractive, the most decent husbands (as you probably have found in more intimate conversation) a certain more or less rationalized stupidity when it comes to the question of women's role in science and government — a fanatic refusal to try to understand, which can only be explained as an expression of an underlying panic. In comparison, the fathers of ambitious women are not such a problem, or so we heard yesterday.

If, as has often been said, the lack of available women in some areas constitutes more of a problem than the lack of available jobs, I think that one reason is to be found in whatever the prejudices of men are against an expansion of women's role in these fields, prejudices, as I have said, that only reinforce what the women themselves feel. The fact is that there is always a historical lag between any emancipation and the inner adjustment of the emancipated. It takes a much longer time to emancipate what goes on deep down inside us — that is, whatever prejudices and inequalities have managed to become part of our impulse life and our identity formation — than the time it takes to redefine professed values and to change legalities. And any part of mankind that has had to accept its self-definition from a more dominant group is apt to define itself by what it is *not* supposed to be. Thus, it is easy to impress on the working women of some classes and pursuits the proposition that they should not be unfeminine, or unmaternal, or unladylike, all of which may well come in conflict with that identity element in many successfully intellectual women whose background decreed that, above all, they should not be unintelligent. It is, then, not enough, as has been said, to be "changing with the changing forces." One must become part of a force that guides change, and this with a reasonably good conscience.

The first step toward this may well be a consideration of whether the working world, where it has been exclusively shaped by men for men, and especially where it has succumbed to the stereotypy of competition, is *really* so conducive to the male sense of continuity in work, home, and citizenship. This cannot be separated from the other, here more basic, consideration, that of the continuity between what woman has always been and always will be; what she is not and never will be; and what she yet can and will become. Permit me to continue in a somewhat personal vein and not to become involved at this point in more than one or two theoretical questions. Since my article on womanhood and in fact the whole special issue of *Daedalus* on "Women in America Today" has been recommended to you, I shall restrict myself to a few further remarks concerning prevalent emotional and intellectual attitudes toward questions of a psychological nature.

I have not made a secret of the fact that it is not easy for a man to discuss sexual differences. My article gives some reasons for this. Prejudice blinds us most of all to the fact that prejudice and blindness exist. Nor do women make it easy for men: whenever we come to consider some difference as vital and essential, we are suspected of inventing new rationalizations for the age-old claim that the proper places for women are the bedroom, the nursery, and the kitchen — in whatever order. Any mention of the lasting function and importance of sexual differences is quickly taken to mean a renewed emphasis on inequality or a reactionary insistence that women should keep their place as defined by men. But if I insist on talking about certain differences, it is because I feel strongly that it is no longer the self-preservation of either sex that is at stake but the preservation of the race. Technological and political developments make it necessary that women should take their place firmly in the sciences as well as in the politics of the future.

But here the question arises: how can we agree, or productively disagree, about women's potentials — we as men and women, and we as workers in different disciplines? Let me illustrate this problem by returning to my article in *Daedalus*. The article consists of some reflections on womanhood, which were presented at the American Academy of Arts and Sciences as part of an interdisciplinary symposium. In my paper, I presented some old observations concerning the different ways in which boys and girls use the spatial dimension in imaginative productions, and discussed the conclusion that, in boys, exterior space and its traversion with speed and energy has a certain pervasive importance, whereas girls emphasize arrangements in which people and animals are contained in enclosures. I related these basic tendencies to the anatomical "inner space," the space in which each human being is "born," and which he progressively exchanges for the extended inner spaces of the mother's arms and watchful presence, and of the home's protective milieu. Nothing in human life is purely biological, however, and it is clear that the basic fact and configuration of the inner space and its extensions has been variously elaborated by cultures and religions which, in fact, under the guise of protecting that sanctum, used it to justify a series of more-or-less strict "confinements," out of which modern woman is only slowly being released. It is, therefore, more than understandable that anything a man says that seems to give new reasons for new confinements, is at first resented, and that even rather far-fetched conclusions, quite foreign to the observer, are drawn, in order to test where behavioral generalizations may lead. There was, for example, a brilliant paper that raised some otherwise valid methodological objections to my work. "Are we to conclude," it was asked, "that women might be set to work on the interior of the atom but not on a frontier subject like emission of radioactivity?" Undoubtedly we men, in turn, are too easily offended by this kind of humor. My main point had been that, where the confinements are broken, women may yet be expected to cultivate the implications of what is biologically and anatomically given. She may, in new areas of activity, balance man's indiscriminate endeavor to perfect his dominion over the outer spaces of national and technological expansion (at the cost of hazarding the annihilation of the species) with the determination to emphasize such varieties of caring and caretaking as would take responsibility for each individual child born in a planned humanity.

I mention this in order to point to a universal difficulty in discussions both intersexual and interdisciplinary. We humans are such moral creatures that we invariably react to any generalization regarding *human* behavior, not with questions of method alone but with questions of immediate applicability to conduct. Natural science escapes this dilemma because it has clear rules of verification confirming what *is*, rather than what should or should not be. You (speaking of you now as natural scientists) would not permit behavioral scientists to say in a discussion of relativity, "Are we to conclude, then, that we should act as if all conduct were relative?" Now, no doubt, the discovery of relativity is part of an emerging world view in which human conduct, too, will be re-evaluated; but this was no part of Einstein's intention. Statements concerning human behavior, however, always seem to be saying something that is equally accessible to the untrained eye and to ordinary commonsense, and that is therefore open to immediate translation into pat rules of conduct. Yet, in our so-called behavioral fields, too, the relation of epistemology to conduct is highly complex, and can be discussed only in searching interdisciplinary work — not in addresses. You can see again why I would hope for further meetings.

In conclusion, however, let me offer you a kind of formula for a review of sex differences. If you happen to read my paper, you will see that it strives (within the methodology of my field) to restore as the most positive anatomical specificity of womanhood what is (all too cursorily, of course) referred to as the "inner space," and to establish as more peripheral those "exterior" anatomical differences that have been utilized through the ages as a criterion of female inferiority. But even if, by doing so, I seem to reaffirm woman's central role in the bearing and upbringing of children and the central role of this task in every woman's experience (whether or not she chooses to become a mother), I must add that everybody, besides being a *body,* is *somebody:* a *person* and a *social being* occupying certain roles as worker and citizen. These three categories constitute "the stuff" that is to be "kept together."

Most verifiable sex differences (beyond those intrinsic to sexuality and procreation) establish for each sex only a range of attitudes and attributes which to most of its members "come naturally," that is, are dispositions, predilections, and inclinations. Many of these could, of course, be unlearned or relearned with more or less effort and special talent. This is not to be denied; with ever-increasing choices given her by the grace of technology and enlightenment, the question is only how much and which parts of her inborn inclinations the woman of tomorrow will feel it most natural to preserve and to cultivate — with "natural" defined in human terms as what can be integrated and made continuous in the three basic aspects mentioned.

As a body, then, woman passes through stages of life that are interlinked with the lives of those whose bodily existence is (increasingly so according to her *own choice*) interdependent with hers. But as a worker, say, in a field structured by mathematical laws, woman is as responsible as any man for criteria of evidence that are intersexual or, better, suprasexual. As an individual person, finally, she utilizes her (biologically given) inclinations and her (technologically and politically given) opportunities to make the decisions that would seem to render her life most continuous and meaningful, without failing the chosen tasks of motherhood and citizenship. The question is how these three areas of life reach into each other — certainly not without conflict and tension and yet with some continuity of purpose.

What I would have to say, then, is not at variance with the assertion that the core of engineering and science is well removed from the workers' sex differences, even as also scientific training is more-or-less peripheral to the intimate tasks of womanhood and motherhood. With you, I am reasonably sure that computers built by women would not betray a female logic (although I do not know how reasonable this reasonableness is, since women did not care to invent them in the first place). The logic of the computers is, for better or for worse, of a suprasexual kind. But what to ask and what not to ask the monsters, and when to trust or not to trust them with vital decisions — there, for example, I would think well-trained women might well contribute to a new kind of vision, in the differential application of scientific thinking to humanitarian tasks.

But I would go further. Do we and can we really know what will happen to science if and when women are truly represented in it — not by a few glorious exceptions, but in the rank and file of the scientific elite? Is scientific inspiration really so impersonal and method-bound that personality plays no role in scientific creativity? And if we grant that a woman is never not a woman, even if and especially when she has become an excellent scientist and co-worker beyond all special apologies or claims, then why deny so strenuously that there may be in science also (on the scientific periphery of some tasks, and maybe in the very core of others) areas where the addition, to the male kind of creative vision, of women's vision and creativity may yet lead, not to new laws of verification, but to new areas of inquiry and to new applications? Such a possibility, I suggest, can be tested only if and when women are sufficiently represented in the sciences so that woman's mind may relax about the task and the role and apply itself to the unknown. Is this really so utopian? If I were a scientist I would at any rate not be dissuaded from such a possibility by the statistical facts that have been presented to us regarding the still very small number of women in science and technology.

As I say this I realize, of course, that our hope lies in a future in which the differential contributions of one sex or another will not be specifiable at all. Here as elsewhere, then, in reaffirming the differences between the sexes I am only trying to disclaim an assumed *sameness* which should not be needed as an argument for *equality* in the first place; and to assert instead an *equivalence* which in many areas of activity has not had a chance to assert itself. In recognizing and developing shared logic and method, we shall be able to reassess with less defensiveness those areas in which sexual differences not only should not be denied but should be affirmed and cultivated.

Whatever economic facts may support the claim that in some areas there is not enough work for either sex as things now are — and whatever practical reasons seem to stand in the way of a contemporaneous development of motherhood and advanced workmanship in those women who choose both — one thing is certain: one reneges on freedoms that one has already grasped only at the risk of becoming illogical or unjust. Circumstances may call on all our inventiveness in new joint adjustments to changing conditions, but they do not excuse prejudices which keep half of mankind from participating in planning and decision-making and this at a time when the other half, by its competitive escalation and acceleration of technological progress, has brought us all to the gigantic brink on which we live with all our affluence.

I have said more about old resistances and prejudices than about the hope that lies in a new era. Yet new strength of adaptation develops in those historical eras in which there is a confluence of emancipated individual resources with the potentials of a new technical and social order. Whether there is any true progress in this world, or only a periodical reintegration of human forces following social conflagrations and technical breakthroughs, may be debatable. But I think I know that new generations gain the full measure of their vitality in the continuity of new freedoms with a developing technology and a historical vision. There, also, personal synthesis is strengthened and with it an increased sense of humanity, which, when it occurs in a woman, even her husband or boyfriend will understand and her children will feel, even if new adjustments are demanded of them too. Social inventiveness and new knowledge can help plan such adjustments in a society that is sure of its values. But without these values, behavioral science has little to offer.

So my conclusion would be that, only when you women come into your own, so will the men, and so will your children.

INDEX

THE M.I.T. PRESS PAPERBACK SERIES

1 **Computers and the World of the Future** edited by Martin Greenberger
2 **Experiencing Architecture** by Steen Eiler Rasmussen
3 **The Universe** by Otto Struve
4 **Word and Object** by Willard Van Orman Quine
5 **Language, Thought, and Reality** by Benjamin Lee Whorf
6 **The Learner's Russian-English Dictionary** by B. A. Lapidus and S. V. Shevtsova
7 **The Learner's English-Russian Dictionary** by S. Folomkina and H. Weiser
8 **Megalopolis** by Jean Gottmann
9 **Time Series** by Norbert Wiener
10 **Lectures on Ordinary Differential Equations** by Witold Hurewicz
11 **The Image of the City** by Kevin Lynch
12 **The Sino-Soviet Rift** by William E. Griffith
13 **Beyond the Melting Pot** by Nathan Glazer and Daniel Patrick Moynihan
14 **A History of Western Technology** by Friedrich Klemm
15 **The Dawn of Astronomy** by Norman Lockyer
16 **Information Theory** by Gordon Raisbeck
17 **The Tao of Science** by R. G. H. Siu
18 **A History of Civil Engineering** by Hans Straub
19 **Ex-Prodigy** by Norbert Wiener
20 **I Am a Mathematician** by Norbert Wiener
21 **The New Architecture and the Bauhaus** by Walter Gropius
22 **A History of Mechanical Engineering** by Aubrey F. Burstall
23 **Garden Cities of To-Morrow** by Ebenezer Howard
24 **Brett's History of Psychology** edited by R. S. Peters
25 **Cybernetics** by Norbert Wiener
26 **Biological Order** by Andre Lwoff
27 **Nine Soviet Portraits** by Raymond A. Bauer
28 **Reflexes of the Brain** by I. Sechenov
29 **Thought and Language** by L. S. Vygotsky
30 **Chinese Communist Society: The Family and the Village** by C. K. Yang
31 **The City: Its Growth, Its Decay, Its Future** by Eliel Saarinen
32 **Scientists as Writers** edited by James Harrison
33 **Candidates, Issues, and Strategies: A Computer Simulation of the 1960 and 1964 Presidential Elections** by I. de S. Pool, R. P. Abelson, and S. L. Popkin
34 **Nationalism and Social Communication** by Karl W. Deutsch
35 **What Science Knows About Life: An Exploration of Life Sources** by Heinz Woltereck
36 **Enzymes** by J. B. S. Haldane
37 **Universals of Language** edited by Joseph H. Greenberg
38 **The Psycho-Biology of Language: An Introduction to Dynamic Philology** by George Kingsley Zipf
39 **The Nature of Metals** by Bruce A. Rogers
40 **Mechanics, Molecular Physics, Heat, and Sound** by R. A. Millikan, D. Roller, and E. C. Watson
41 **North American Trees** by Richard J. Preston, Jr.
42 **God and Golem, Inc.** by Norbert Wiener
43 **The Architecture of H. H. Richardson and His Times** by Henry-Russell Hitchcock
44 **Toward New Towns for America** by Clarence Stein
45 **Man's Struggle for Shelter in an Urbanizing World** by Charles Abrams
46 **Science and Economic Development** by Richard L. Meier
47 **Human Learning** by Edward Thorndike
48 **Pirotechnia** by Vannoccio Biringuccio
49 **A Theory of Natural Philosophy** by Roger Joseph Boscovich
50 **Bacterial Metabolism** by Marjory Stephenson
51 **Generalized Harmonic Analysis** and **Tauberian Theorems** by Norbert Wiener
52 **Nonlinear Problems in Random Theory** by Norbert Wiener
53 **The Historian and the City** edited by Oscar Handlin and John Burchard
54 **Planning for a Nation of Cities** edited by Sam Bass Warner, Jr.
55 **Silence** by John Cage
56 **New Directions in the Study of Language** edited by Eric H. Lenneberg
57 **Prelude to Chemistry** by John Read
58 **The Origins of Invention** by Otis T. Mason
59 **Style in Language** edited by Thomas A. Sebeok
60 **World Revolutionary Elites** edited by Harold D. Lasswell and Daniel Lerner
61 **The Classical Language of Architecture** by John Summerson
62 **China Under Mao** edited by Roderick MacFarquhar
63 **London: The Unique City** by Steen Eiler Rasmussen
64 **The Search for the Real** by Hans Hofmann
65 **The Social Function of Science** by J. D. Bernal
66 **The Character of Physical Law** by Richard Feynman
67 **No Peace for Asia** by Harold R. Isaacs
68 **The Moynihan Report and the Politics of Controversy** by Lee Rainwater and William L. Yancey
69 **Communism in Europe,** Vol. I, edited by William E. Griffith
70 **Communism in Europe,** Vol. II, edited by William E. Griffith
71 **The Rise and Fall of Project Camelot** edited by Irving L. Horowitz